Empowered

A Teacher Tale of Classroom Culture Creation

Nathan Cureton

Copyright © 2014 Nathan Cureton
All rights reserved.

ISBN: 1500482633
ISBN 13: 9781500482633

Dedicated to all who teach,
for you are the heroes of our generation.

AND

To Kim, the hero of my all.

Table of Contents

Author's Note		vii
Introduction to the Guiding Principles of Culture Creating		xi
Chapter One	Crashed at the Crossroads	1
Chapter Two	Sheri and the Principle of High Expectations	8
Chapter Three	Alex and the Principle of Relationships of Respect and Trust	47
Chapter Four	Paul and the Principle of Reinforcing the Positive	89
Chapter Five	Trisha and the Principle of Student-Centered Instruction	135
Chapter Six	The Crossroads Traversed	187
Counselor Kris's Cliff Notes	The Guiding Principles of Culture Creating	191
About the Author		203

Author's Note

Painting and Shaping – A Teacher's Calling

A white canvas stares back at the painter, empty yet willing. Its potential is limitless in the hand of the expert artist. All the canvas needs is for the painter to create with it what he will, manipulating each color and blending each stroke to transform the blank canvas into the masterpiece it was destined to become.

A student walks through the classroom door on the first day of school, excited yet apprehensive. His potential is every bit as limitless in the hand of the master teacher. However, this student arrives without the benefit of being a pure, blank slate. He may be spotted with poor habits or blemished from a difficult home. He may be splattered by laziness or hindered with a disability. Yet still, the teacher is expected to transform this stained canvas into a masterpiece. The challenge is as real as it is daunting.

Yet while the canvas, clean and pure, is incapable of painting itself, the tarnished student carries a distinct advantage – the ability of self-transformation. While the painter is solely responsible for his masterpiece, the teacher is not. Instead, he is privileged to work side by side with his student, guiding him toward that which he is destined to become.

Principle Based Instruction

Sounds grandiose, right? Where might a teacher even begin to tackle such a lofty target, a target we are expected to collectively accomplish for innumerable students from countless backgrounds with varying needs? The education community does not lack for concrete methods, with ideas as numerous as the students we teach. Yet, what may work for one student may not for another, for each canvas comes pre-blotted in its own unique style.

This challenge presses teachers to innovate strategies to accommodate each and every student need. While some students may need to go fast, others slow. Some may need consistent scaffolding, others independence. Some may need more audio, others visual, others kinesthetic. The never-ending array of philosophies and fads may both confuse and overwhelm, not to mention underperform. So, what teachers need is to comprehend a universal framework for applying all those ideas and methods; they need a tool belt for all these tools.

Empowered: A Teacher Tale of Classroom Culture Creation teaches four universal principles that are advantageous to all students when properly applied. It purposely and strategically neglects detailed lists of concrete strategies, for as useful as such strategies may be, they yield little lasting results when implemented outside a principle-based framework. Should I use a seating chart? Will this new technology help? How should I address this misbehaving student? These and countless other concrete questions are better answered through a principle-based lens. Thus, teachers should first learn the framework principles, then apply them in accordance with the unique needs of individual communities, schools, classrooms, and students.

Why a Novel?

As helpful as the explicit delineation of the principles might be, it is in the application of the principles that the painting takes shape. *Empowered* illustrates the four guiding principles by modeling them through the eyes of the teachers and students at East Crossroads Middle School. As you read, you'll observe the learning process of individual teachers as they discover and apply each principle, subsequently enjoying the positive effects their change has on students.

Plus, quite frankly, who doesn't enjoy a good novel? Applying these principles to a fictionalized setting increases enjoyment while demonstrating concrete applications. After all, a spoonful of sugar does help the medicine go down.

How Can I Best Use This Book?

Ultimately, *Empowered* has three primary purposes: educate, entertain, and motivate. The story itself rests upon the foundation of the four principles explicitly detailed in the "Cliff Notes" section located on pages 191-202, briefly introduced beginning on the next page, and spotlighted throughout the narrative. Either review the Cliff Notes before beginning the novel itself, or if you're anxious to get right to the story, peek back at the Cliff Notes simultaneous with reading. Either approach, or a combination of the two, will enable you to connect the principle to its application, making the book more worthwhile and influential to your own teaching.

Classroom Culture Creation contains four main chapters sandwiched between a short introduction and conclusion. Each main chapter explores the journey of a single teacher struggling to learn and implement one of the four principles. Each character is stereotypical to an extreme so you can better relate to their circumstances, facilitating your own learning and application. Yes, few teachers actually behave as extreme as these, but it is in their extremities that the principle can be taught and we can self-identify. So, look for yourself in each character, and the principles will come to life.

Each main chapter concludes with a brief author's note that explores significant applications. Each author's note also includes a series of personal application questions for your consideration. This process of reflection and application will personalize the principles and strengthen your efforts to become as the master painter, creating your own classroom culture of success for your student canvases of limitless potential.

Introduction to the Guiding Principles of Culture Creating

Purpose and Overview of Culture Creating

Every student to ever walk into a classroom is accompanied by an inseparable gift – choice. This ability is made manifest in their behavior, attention, and effort. Though we may discipline poor behavior, they may still poke their neighbor with a pencil. Though we may raise our voice to maintain attention, they may still remain lost in a hazy daydream. Though we may motivate with great enthusiasm, they may still neglect their homework. As much as teachers painstakingly strive to guide students in the proper direction, at the end of the day, it is the students themselves who must choose whether or not to follow. We cannot force them. Thus, this gift of choice enables students to pursue for themselves a path of success, mediocrity, or failure.

So, what is a teacher to do? If students are able to veer from the course we lead, how do we get them to follow? How do we fulfill the duties of our position?

A wise teacher will shun the temptation to disregard student choice. Instead of striving to force our will with coercion, bribes, or wishful pleading – usually producing the opposite effect we desire – we must embrace each student's agency and use it for their ultimate good. Instead of working against their ability to choose, we must work with it. We must help them help themselves. We must build a classroom culture where students are empowered to accept responsibility for their own learning and choose for themselves the path of success.

How does one create a classroom culture of success?

Because all teachers and students are unique, so should be the dynamics of each classroom's culture. The high school class should be different from the elementary, the inner city from the rural, and gifted and talented from special education. Similarly, two neighboring classes within the same school must unavoidably function with a culture all their own, for the makeup of individual students and their teacher are still unique. Thus, the details of any classroom culture should be flexible, fluid, and dependent upon the needs of the class.

And while unique in practice, there are common guiding principles that provide the framework within which details should flow in all given settings. Outlined in detail in the Cliff Notes section on pages 191-202, these guiding principles are:

- <u>High Expectations</u>: Academic and behavioral expectations are challenging, clearly defined, regularly communicated, and consistently reinforced.
- <u>Relationships of Respect and Trust</u>: Teacher relationships with individual students are built on professionalism and friendliness for the purpose of building intrinsic motivation.
- <u>Reinforcing the Positive</u>: Desired student behavior is reinforced by ignoring inconsequential behavior, recognizing desired behavior, and properly addressing consequential misbehavior.
- <u>Student-Centered Instruction</u>: Instructional methods focus on the needs of individual students for the ultimate goal of individual student success.

Though separate by definition, the application of these principles weave together in unity to create a classroom culture that both empowers and motivates students to choose success for themselves.

Student Benefits

Ultimately, our goal goes beyond their success in our classroom. Yes, we'd love all A's on their research reports, but above that, we want to develop the habit of A-like outcomes in all they do throughout life. We want learning to become a pleasure and success a way of life, not just a fleeting flirtation.

If students choose to fully partake of your classroom culture, the effects bear fruit in numerous ways. Self-motivation increases, personal responsibility and accountability strengthen, and priorities realign. They forget their fear of the process of success and become willing to put in the work. They become a positive influence on others, whether by word or deed. And ultimately, they develop the habits necessary to better fulfill their ultimate role as productive members of society.

Teacher Benefits

A classroom culture of success is beneficial to teachers by enabling them to concentrate on prevention rather than the endless cycle of reaction. Where reactionary systems play catch up, a culture of success is step ahead. There's no need to address student chatter because it doesn't happen; no need to help a student with missing homework because it's all turned in; no need to track down a student to retake a test because they've already come to you. You've created the culture in which they accomplish these things of their own accord. It's behavior management without managing behavior.

Yet, when all is said and done, the primary benefit a teacher enjoys in creating a classroom culture of success is the personal satisfaction of influencing a student's life. For why did we become teachers in the first place? The stacks of papers to grade? That parent who yelled at us last week? No, we are teachers for a singular, ultimate end, a purpose that drives us to endure the burdensome periphery to enjoy the main attraction, a narrowed focus that motivates us to serve beyond ourselves – we love kids.

Chapter One

Crashed at the Crossroads

"**H**ere we go again!"

It was late August and the first day of another school year at East Crossroads Middle School. Kris Able, the new school counselor, took her first step into the teachers' lounge to the unfortunate welcome of this ominous exclamation. With her lunch in hand, she stopped just inside the doorframe to scan the scene before her. Large white walls hovered over the room's inhabitants, with sound boards strategically mounted throughout to contain the contents of the conversations within. Base cabinetry and countertop lined the walls, with papers and supplies strewn about as evidence of last minute scrambling. Windowless, the room's humming florescent lights were encased with blue plastic coverings struggling to resemble the bright summer sky and failing to ameliorate the gloomy situation.

Kris observed the groups of teachers collected together around the mismatched assortment of round tables. Some gathered with forced smiles, trying to make the best of the body blows they'd endured from the day's first four classes. Others, scattered about the outer tables, quietly ate their lunch in solitude, methodically crunching on miniature ice cubes from the ice machine benevolently bestowed upon the staff as last year's Christmas bonus. While a few even openly commiserated about the upcoming nine months of doom.

Quickly assessing her new surroundings, Kris mentally summarized in a single word the lounge's collective feeling – stress. She'd seen it before, and she saw it again now. She saw it in their shadowy eyes and slumped shoulders. She saw it in their forced smiles and shrill voices. Though outwardly manifesting their inner stress in varying ways, it was evident that all were coping with the burden of transition from a lazy summer and recovery from an arduous first day. They looked much like their own rewarmed leftovers.

Kris ultimately found a seat at an empty table along the back wall and began munching on her Caesar salad. Her graceful hand grasped a fork, the firmness of her grip demonstrating her self-confidence and awareness. Her large, green eyes were mysterious when lost in thought yet penetrating when focused. Her straight, auburn hair could blend in with her surroundings while her cheerful, regular smile shined bright in a crowd. Always professional yet pleasant, Kris carried herself with the dignity of royalty crossed with the humility of an apprentice.

From the back of the teachers' lounge, Kris couldn't help but overhear snippets of conversations from the varying groups of teachers. She zeroed in on one such conversation, or better defined as a monologue, as it evoked a feeling quite different than the others. The positive energy and unnatural volume from the first year English teacher, Ms. Sheri Price, pierced the surrounding haze of anxiety.

"...I mean, really! How totally cool! I've been training for this for, like, the last four years, my whole life really, and now my dream has become a reality. My first day as a teacher! It's been awesome! Well, I guess I had a rough few classes today, but it's the first day; it's going to be great! I've got so many ideas, and tomorrow I plan to..."

"...You plan to tone it down?"

Mr. Paul Lowry bluntly interrupted from a neighboring table. The grumpy old science teacher was in no mood for such blind orations of cheer, for he himself, the voice of the initial lamentation Kris encountered upon entering the lounge, was amidst an oration all his own, except of a much different tone.

"These kids seem to get worse with each passing year," Paul moaned. "Parents raise them to be slugs and then expect us to transform them into scholars. Impossible. We might as well line them up and knock them down like the bowling pins that they are."

A voice perked up from the opposite side of the lounge, "More bowling analogies, Paul? You're as sad as the 130 game you averaged this summer."

"That's 230, Little Miss Trish," retorted Paul. "I could break 200 wearing those three-inch heels of yours. You'd think a distinguished mathematician and two-time Teacher of the Year, like yourself, could count by hundreds. Perhaps admin should rethink their decision at the year-end banquet."

"That's three-time Teacher of the Year. And you're welcome to my high heels any time, just return them with disinfectant, would you?"

Mrs. Trisha LaValle couldn't help but begin the year as the previous had ended. Her big-sister rivalry with Paul was the only reason she ever set foot in the lowly teachers' lounge. The entertainment of their not-so-friendly banter had amused her for years, and she wasn't about to stop stepping on his toes now when it still produced such humorous retaliations.

Kris silently shook her head from her back table. Yes, she'd seen this before, and yes, it bothered her then as well. She knew this room was full of promising teachers with great potential to influence students, some of whom just seemed to have become lost in daily grind.

I might be counseling more than students this year, Kris thought to herself.

Soon thereafter, Kris was interrupted from her thoughts by the entrance of a tall, young beanpole whose floppy feet expanded out of necessity to support his gangly frame. He sported an archaic, distinct part on the right side of his strawberry-blond hair which was further accentuated by an uncomfortable smile. His freckly cheeks and wiry torso resembled something similar to a giraffe.

The conversations quickly died down at the presence of an administrator in the teachers' lounge. And as awkward as Mr. Nate Phippen was, to the teachers, he was still one of "them."

"Hello… uh, I mean… good afternoon, everyone. Small message… uh, announcement for you. We'd like to have a brief… uh, short… faculty meeting right after school. Let's gather… uh, meet… in the library."

Upon Mr. Phippen's exit from his brief visit to enemy territory, Kris observed a collective groan from the group along with a smattering of irritated exclamations, the most prominent of which coming from Paul.

Yep. I think I'll be counseling more than students this year.

—m—

The halls were filling with students, making their way from lunch to fifth period, as Kris exited the teachers' lounge. She blended in with the flow of students, heading downstream toward their mandated ponds of learning. The groups of students differed as much as the schools of fish they resembled. To Kris's right strode a pod of trout: calm, confident, and compliant. To her left she spotted a huddle of gold fish, the bright overachievers who reveled in being the teachers' pets. A ways in front of her, Kris spied the bright colors of the school's crew from the tropics, clearly prioritizing attracting attention above all else. And Kris didn't even have to turn around to identify the group of clown fish behind her; their rowdy cackling at the expense of some nerdy sardines was evidence enough.

As she continued downstream, Kris found herself caught behind a couple of blowfish blubbering about the woes of another year.

"Here we go again, back for another round in this dump of a school. You ready for another year of torture?"

"Man, two years was bad enough. And if things keep goin' like today, our last year'll be the worst yet."

"Yeah, it's like juvy. We're sentenced to suffer when our only crime was livin'."

"I know, man. It's like our teachers are the cops and Mr. Phippen's the warden."

"And Mr. Lowry's the executioner. I swear, that old man'll kill you from either boredom or yelling. The only thing that kept me awake in his class was the occasional insult he squawked my way."

"The guy's a total nut job, man. And do you have history with Mr. Clemmington, the football coach? The dude's about as smart as pigskin."

Eventually, Kris was able to swim around and scurry off toward her counseling office. While in route, she couldn't help but notice the similarity between this student conversation and those she overheard in the teachers' lounge moments earlier. Misguided. Pessimistic. Both teacher and student seemed to be swimming the same course, the irony being that neither desired their ultimate destination nor did they enjoy their travel partners. They were all suckerfish, latched on to the very things they despised.

Kris's thoughts drifted back to the lounge where some of her colleagues were sure to be stalling their return to class. She could almost hear Paul's voice rising above the rest, leading the rant against his unfortunate circumstances, subjecting any who disagreed to his cynical grumbling. *"Another year of agony,"* he'd probably be saying. *"Another year in a dark alley with no bowling ball to amuse me. Instead we're subjected to..."*

"...another year of pubescent teenagers more worried about the cute girl across the room than the assignment on their desks." Paul, savoring the last few minutes of his lunch break, completed Kris's imaginative comments to the few who lingered.

"I feel sorry for the rest of you," continued Paul from the high horse of his black, plastic chair, crunching ice with his stern jaw. "I've only got one more year to endure, then I'll be set free to relish in the word I've craved for decades – retirement. Yes folks, another year and the king will be put out to pasture. Lazy mornings, reading the news, bowling leagues..."

"...Sleepin' 'till noon, hangin' with the girls, and freedom from all teachers!" The two boys Kris had previously overheard continued their lamentations as they lapped the hallways.

"Nine months until summer vacation," the boys complained. "Nine months until we're done with this dump. But the problem is that nine months..."

"...is a long time" mourned Paul, unknowingly finishing the students' line. "That still means nine months of lesson plans, papers to grade, and students to manage. I hope I can..."

"...make it that long. It's gonna be brutal, man. It's gonna be..."

"...terribly challenging to endure. But..."

"...like it or not..."
"...here we go again!"

Kris banked right through an open doorway to a quaint, welcoming reception area. To the right of the doorway stretched a narrow set of ceiling to floor windows connecting the office area to the stream of students in the hallway. By the wall opposite the windows stood an L-shaped receptionist desk complete with a computer, desk calendar, water bottle, and some framed family photos. Four red cloth chairs were paired off in twos, the first facing the desk with their backs to the windows and the second adjacent along the connecting wall. In the corner stood a small, decorative table with a live Peace Lily plant sitting on top, enjoying the sky blue walls as if spring itself were alive within.

Another wall held a series of display trays, hung horizontally, holding various pamphlets for public perusal. Above the trays in bold, black vinyl lettering proclaimed, "Welcome to The Counselor Corner."

The entire room smiled with empathy, beckoning those in need to partake of the support offered within. Kris stepped passed the entrance toward another door just beyond the reception area. She entered her office, leaving the door open behind her, and curled around an executive-style desk to the comfort of her black, rolling chair. She breathed in deeply, surveyed the contents of her office, and released the pressure in her lungs with a sigh.

The feel of Kris's office was similar to the reception area. The only oddity was the positioning of the large white leather chairs situated in front of her desk. There were three of them, two on one side facing one on the other, separated by a small circular wood table with a round ceramic dish perched on top containing an assortment of fruity candy. In a traditional office situation, one might expect chairs to face the desk; however, Kris was anything but traditional. She had strategically arranged her office so as to facilitate ease of conversation as equals, shunning the situational superiority created by conversation separated by a desk.

From her seat, Kris looked toward the open doorway leading to the reception area. Her eyes then traced backward to the leather chairs and wood table, the candy left untouched as if waiting for someone in need of encouragement to loosen their tongue. Deep in thought, her gaze then followed the line back up to her desk and over to her computer monitor in the corner. She clicked a button and began to type.

Journal Entry – August 24

I'm nearing the end of my first day at East Crossroads and as a school counselor. After fifteen years of teaching, it's hard not being in the classroom enjoying the kids. And though the quiet of my office has felt a little lonely, I'm confident things will pick up shortly. I'm still excited to be a positive influence on students in this new role.

And yet, I also perceive that there are some adults in our school who could use some positive influence as well. Honestly, much of the negativity is probably attributable to the stresses of the first day; I remember feeling a bit overwhelmed at the beginning of every year I taught. So as the year progresses, perhaps an opportunity will present itself to help a teacher or two.

Chapter Two

Sheri and the Principle of High Expectations

"Hello... uh, good morning, Kris."

Mr. Phippen tracked down the new counselor in the hallway before the rush of a new school week began. The stomping of his size fourteens announced his approach well before his voice. After a brief exchange of pleasantries, Kris gently prodded the assistant principal as to the purpose of his visit.

> <u>High Expectations</u> – "Academic and behavioral expectations are challenging, clearly defined, regularly communicated, and consistently reinforced."

"Oh... uh, yes," Mr. Phippen stuttered, grateful for the reminder. "I'm worried about a new student. I've heard some reports that he's struggling... uh, transitioning poorly."

"Could this be Seth, the eighth grader who moved in late last week?" Kris questioned. After a nod of confirmation, she continued. "Yes, when I met with him and his sister before his first day, I could tell he might have a hard time with the change."

"It appears your worry was right. I was hoping... uh, I'd like to ask, that you keep an eye on him. He could probably use a little guidance... uh, counseling."

"I'd be happy to. I think I'd like to first observe his behavior in class, and then I'll have a better idea of how I can best help. Thanks for pointing that out, Mr. Phippen; it looks like you've got a perceptive eye!"

"Well... uh, thanks," stammered Mr. Phippen, a little unsure of how to take the compliment. "Have a... uh, nice day." With an uneasy smile and childish fidget, he turned on his heel and made his way back in the direction he had come, a single stride reaching the length of two of most others.

Patiently waiting for the conclusion of first period, Kris leaned against the wall just outside the language arts classroom of the first year teacher, Ms. Sheri Price. And though she waited outside so as to not be a disturbance, the perpetual clamor Kris heard within would have certainly concealed an unexpected entry. For behind the closed door echoed a consistent low rumble of student chatter, like the pitter-patter of raindrops against an overhead roof. Each droplet of an individual voice blended together to create a single roll of rainfall which ebbed and flowed with the shifting mood of the storm, the rising waters building pressure.

As imperceptible as a dull breeze failing to repel the storm, Kris noticed a faint, high-pitched voice in the background, dulled by the swirling blanketing elements. The voice garbled encouragement and requested compliance, as if Mother Nature would actually hearken to a mere "please." This sputtering wind was ruthlessly blunted by the sheer number and repetition of the raindrops. And as the dismissal bell neared, Kris feared that the mounting flood might sweep Ms. Price away.

And then mercifully, with the ring of the bell, the dam broke and the waters came rushing out into the hallway. Kris waited for the torrent to pass before stepping into the room. Across the way, on the opposite side of class, stood the dejected teacher, still trying to catch her breath while soaked with feelings of inadequacy. Sheri's countenance told Kris that her heart was true, but she was all too unprepared for her first year of teaching.

"Good morning! It's Ms. Price, right?" Kris stepped forward with a friendly wave.

Sheri jumped at the sound of an unanticipated visitor. "Oh! Hello there! Yes, that's right. I'm Sheri, the new language arts teacher."

"It's a pleasure to meet you, Sheri. I'm Kris, the school counselor. This is my first year at East Crossroads as well."

"You too?" Sheri clapped her hands together in celebration. "I'm so glad I'm not the only one! It seems like everyone here is so wise and experienced, and I can't seem to catch up. It's just these kids, I love them to death, but I just don't know what to do. They just keep talking and talking, you know what I mean? They're the sweetest things in the world, but I can't get them to stop talking. They just go on and on and on, no matter what I say…"

"…Well Sheri," Kris politely interjected, smiling at the irony of Sheri's animated rambling, "I am new to East Crossroads, but I'm not new to education. I've actually been a teacher for fifteen years elsewhere, but this is my first year as a counselor, so I do know how it feels to get used to a new role. Change can be challenging."

"Oh, I see. Fifteen years, huh? With all that experience, I bet you learned how to get students to listen. So tell me, what should I do when…"

"…When students begin to enter for second period?" Kris interrupted as the warning bell sounded. "I'd love to talk some things through with you a little later, but as for now, I was just hoping to sit in the back to observe one of your students. We've had a couple concerns expressed, and I just wanted to see how he acts in class before I begin working with him. Is it all right with you if I sit over there for a few minutes?"

At Sheri's affirmation, Kris took her seat as a new deluge of students burst in just before the ring of the tardy bell. Kris spotted Seth, who immediately slumped over asleep in his desk, and she quickly became distracted by the surrounding torrent of energy. While Ms. Price scurried about to ready her materials, the students took full advantage of the opportunity. Chatting, laughing, gossiping, the class maximized their time by minimizing that of their teacher.

"Class. Excuse me. Will you please take your seats?"

Sheri's request fell on deaf ears, so she gathered her wits, put on a smile, and tried again.

"Hey! Students! It's time to begin!" She hollered with a sing-song tone of forced politeness. Begrudgingly, the class complied with the screech of wind, calming the rain if but for a short while.

> From 1.1.1 – "Students generally perform to the level of their own expectations, whether high or low."

"Thank you. Now, I'm excited to announce that today we begin our very first writing unit, persuasion!" The pep in Sheri's voice was as natural as it was naïve. "This is the perfect unit for eighth graders because we'll explore the ins and outs of effective argument. You'll learn how quality persuasion enables you to get what you want!"

"Like no school for a month?" A burst of chuckles reverberated at the brazen joke of the overconfident class clown.

Kris noted how Sheri seemed caught off guard by the unwelcome comment. It was clear she didn't know how to address it, so she ended up not addressing it at all. The keen eyes of the students caught hold of this rookie mistake, now more determined to see how far they could push their boundaries.

"Throughout the unit," she continued, "we'll learn different strategies to aid you in the culminating assignment. Each of you will identify something about the school you would like to change and prepare a speech to be hypothetically delivered to Mr. Phippen."

"Only hot girls in eighth grade!"

This time the boys' laughter combined with a few exaggerated gasps of horror from their female counterparts.

Sheri continued onward, separating students into groups to review the assignment summary handout. This generous latitude allowed the pound of rain to swell from a consistent hum to a pounding drum. Sheri bounced about the room making her best effort to calm the storm with reminders and shushes, but to the students, their teacher's hot air lacked substance, so it only added fuel to the fury. Sheri was again caught in the midst of a downpour, completely unable to control the rising waters.

From the back corner of the room, Kris quietly maneuvered her way around the chaos toward the exit on the other side. She had finished observing the sleeping Seth along with his well-intentioned yet beginner teacher. As Kris sneaked into the hallway, she felt compassion and understanding for both the teacher and her students. A first year teacher has to start somewhere; it's just too bad that she was managing a flood instead of merely getting her feet wet.

"Kris, help me!"

Mere moments after the end of school that day, Sheri found herself in the doorway of Kris's office in the Counselor Corner. She braced herself against the metal frame, seeking support from anything willing to intervene.

"You saw my class today. You saw how I couldn't control them. We're in the second week, and it has gotten worse every day. I have so many exciting things I want to do with these kids, but I can't because they won't listen to me. It's like I'm…"

As Sheri continued to decompress, Kris stood up from behind her desk, took Sheri by the arm, and led her over to one of the two paired white leather chairs. Kris then sat in her own on the opposite side, the two being separated by the wood table with the candy dish on top. Kris continued to lend a listening ear, for it was clear that Sheri had a greater need to unload her baggage than upload new advice.

The speech marched on. Sheri's lips curled around each word with impressive pronunciation considering the speed with which they came. Her hands gestured about in an effort to keep pace with her mouth. Her dyed blond hair hung short and bounced around with the movements of her spirited hands. Perspiration beaded around her thin, wire-framed glasses perched atop her rounded nose.

"...You see Kris, this isn't what I dreamed it would be," Sheri, finally slowing down, whispered between gasps. "What can I possibly do to turn this around?"

With some reluctance, she closed her mouth and dropped her eyes, exhausted from the exertion. Kris let her deflated friend take a moment to recover in silence. After some time, Kris reached her hand toward the wood table between them and opened a small drawer on the side facing her.

"You know, this fruity candy seems to do the trick for teenagers, but we adults need something a little better." Kris removed her hand from the drawer to reveal a fun sized KitKat bar. She unwrapped the candy, broke it in half, and reached forward to hand a bar to Sheri. "Chocolate. It may not cure our problems, but it sure can help us cope with them."

Sheri looked at the candy in Kris's outstretched hand. A grateful smile sprung back to her face as she snatched up the offering. Together the two enjoyed their reprieve for a moment, savoring both the taste and the quiet company. Sheri's tense torso sunk into the soft cushions, her muscles now able to relax.

Kris couldn't help but feel empathy for the unwinding stress case before her. It wasn't too long ago that she was in that same situation. She too hadn't anticipated the harsh reality of fulltime teaching. Six classes of thirty plus students, learning disabilities, limited English proficiency, troubled homes, fluctuating hormones (from the students, of course), class clowns, and an endless stream of prepping, grading, and filing. No wonder they had three months off in the summer; they cram twelve months' worth of work into three-quarters of the time.

And what makes matters worse for teachers like Sheri is that they care. They care for kids. Teachers like Sheri are willing to put forth their very best on every aspect of teaching because they want the same from their students. They plan hard, grade thoroughly, accommodate exceptions, and teach with enthusiasm all because they care for kids. Yes, Sheri's heart was true; she just lacked the experience to match her true intentions. And though Kris was now a *student* counselor, how could she possibly shirk an

> From 4.2.3 – A student-centered teacher's primary focus is "guiding students to achieve according to their individual circumstances."

opportunity to assist this clumsy colt with a stallion's potential?

"It looks like you've worked hard to prepare yourself for your first year teaching," Kris observed. "How long have you wanted to be a teacher?" Though Kris knew such an open-ended question would inevitably bring another lengthy disclosure, she was willing.

Sheri jerked upright in her chair at the question. Her excited expression revealed the gist of her answer before it even escaped her mouth. "How long? Forever!" she announced. "Both my parents and three of my four grandparents were teachers. I used to play school with my little brother before I even started kindergarten; I made him sit in a desk while I scribbled on a little toy chalkboard for hours. In elementary school, I was voted most likely to become a teacher three times. In high school I volunteered as a reading aide three days a week and still maintained a 4.0 GPA. In college I only got a 3.95 – those stupid putnet, no Punnett, squares on that genetics midterm! But I always had my eye focused on middle school language arts. I even planned out all my writing units during my sophomore year of college, and I've refined them each summer since – I'm most proud of my poetry unit. I hope I can last until February!"

"Wow! Look at you," Kris intervened. "So to make a long story, well, less long, it seems to me that you've pretty much been destined for this. And now you're finally here!"

"I know! Isn't it… great?" The statement hung on Sheri's lips for an elongated moment. Her mouth still smiled but her eyes retreated behind her glasses as if they didn't fully believe what her lips had just said. "Well, I… at least I want it to be great."

Perceptive and wise, Kris detected Sheri's dipping emotions. After having reached into the drawer of the table, Kris stood and maneuvered to the unoccupied seat next to Sheri. She placed her smooth, confident hand on Sheri's shoulder.

"Sheri, it will be. With a teacher who cares as much as you, there's no other option but to be great. Here, take this."

Kris stood back up and held out her hand to reveal the presence of another KitKat. Sheri looked up at her newfound mentor and stood with a modest smile returning to her face. She took the offering, understanding it meant more than just chocolate.

"Enjoy this as a well-earned reprieve, then come see me tomorrow afternoon. I've got some ideas that should help."

Mrs. Trisha LaValle stood in her flashy high heels, leaning against the teachers' lounge countertop. Her left leg crossed over her right, and she stared down her pointed nose at the pitiful sight before her. Sheri had sounded off to anyone willing to listen, and after several minutes of discharge, Trisha was now regretting having gotten sucked in.

"…When we separated out into groups to prepare for the debate, they seemed to talk about everything else but what they were supposed to. They were to develop their main points of argument, but instead they only argued about their weekend plans! What was I to do?"

Trisha had only intended to lend half an ear to the young fiasco out of sheer pity, but instead Sheri had grabbed both with firm fortitude. If she let this newbie stay latched for long, Trisha feared it could tarnish her distinguished reputation.

"What were you to do?" Paul's demeaning voice interrupted, blaring from the opposite side of the lounge. "Threaten them with their lives. Either that or threaten them with more incessant yakking."

The blatant insult caught Sheri off guard, stopping her marching mouth mid-sentence. Trisha and the other teachers didn't much notice, having become accustomed to Paul's cynicism over the years. Though faltering only temporarily, Sheri quickly recovered and took the jab in stride. She continued her discourse to others seated nearby in hushed undertones.

Trisha spotted her opportunity for escape and slipped away as stealthily as her clacking high heels would take her.

—⚏—

As promised, Kris welcomed Sheri to her office the following afternoon, and true to character, Sheri began by repeating everything she had before, completely unable to hold the flood gates. Yet once ready for discussion, Kris cautiously proceeded, careful to help her colleague stay on course.

"What do you hope to accomplish with your students? What is your ultimate goal?" inquired Kris.

"Good question. Well, learning, I suppose."

"Great. Now, let me ask you. Are they learning?"

Sheri's eyes found their way downward as she could tell where this was going. "Not much," she replied shamefully.

"Why not?"

"Well, they can't hear me say anything."

"So, they can't hear you? Why not? You don't seem to have a problem expressing yourself."

"Kris, they won't listen to me! They're too busy chatting with a neighbor or cracking some joke. How can they hear and learn if I can't even get them to listen?"

"Do they know they're supposed to listen?"

Completely perplexed by the question, Sheri's only response was a look of bewilderment. *Do they know they should listen? Uh, hello? Aren't I teaching eighth grade?*

Kris wasn't fazed by the response, nor was she surprised. She had been going for a shocker to catch Sheri's attention and to emphasize the importance of this first lesson.

Kris proceeded. "You'd like to think that students would come to you understanding the basic expectation of listening. After all, they have been in school for nearly a decade. But the reality is, Sheri, these students must be taught clear expectations in every class every year. Each teacher they have ever had does things differently. Some may permit a bit of chatter when others don't. Some may expect focused group work when others don't. Some may expect raised hands when others don't. When every teacher they have ever had does things differently, how can we expect students to know what you expect of them if you don't tell them?"

Kris paused only a moment before continuing, "And then we add the fact that these are still young teens discovering the world and their independence. The very nature of their age and development propels them to test their limits. And when that limit is undefined, they'll push right through."

> From 1.2.1 – "Within the first week of school, teach all expectations… *explicitly*. Do not assume that students know what is expected."

Sheri stared intently across the way to where Kris sat in her own white leather chair. Her words, as simple as they were, rang true. Had she told her students her expectations? She had shushed and reminded, but no, she hadn't clearly defined how she expected her students to behave. How could they hit a target that they didn't even know existed?

Kris continued, "I like to compare it to popping popcorn, not the microwave kind, but that old-fashioned style of kernel popping in a pot on the stove or open flame. Do you know what I'm talking about?"

"Of course! My dad used to do that when we were young. I loved it with extra butter."

"Yeah, you got it. So, what would happen if you just threw the kernels directly on the burner?"

"Interesting," Sheri mused. "I don't know. If they even popped, they'd probably just burn."

"Either that or pop right onto the floor. Whichever happened, not many of the kernels would be edible. However, what occurs when you heat the kernels within the confines of a pot?"

Sheri thought a moment. "They all pop, and they all stay safe in the container." Her eyes flashed bright once the interpretation clicked. "Oh! So it's the walls of the pot that enable the process to work!"

"Exactly," Kris continued, pleased. "It's the clearly defined boundaries that empower our students to achieve their full potential. If we just throw them right into the fire of the curriculum, they'll spring about in any which way or burn right up where they stand. Limits and expectations create the environment in which they can learn, function, and thrive."

> From 1.1.1 – "As teachers cannot force students to hold themselves to certain expectations, teachers can, however, guide students to adopt those of the teacher."

Encouraged with the significance of what she just learned, Sheri popped right out of her chair and paced the room. Her thoughts raced about while some unknowingly escaped her lips, leaving Kris struggling to interpret the meaning of Sheri's fragmented bursts.

"Expectations. I didn't even! Chatty groups. Too far in. Popcorn. How can I now?"

Just as Sheri's deliberation was reaching a climax, Kris stood and guided Sheri back to her seat, placing a KitKat on the table before her. Sheri complied with a smile, clearly unaware of her innocent overreaction. As she sunk back down with a mouth full of chocolate, Kris took advantage of the opportunity.

"I think you're beginning to see. It's every teacher's individual responsibility to create a classroom environment most conducive to student success. The kernels won't pop on their own, and they won't pop right in the wrong environment. You must build the appropriate environment, and it all begins with your expectations."

"I think I get it," responded Sheri as she crunched her last bite, "but we're already two weeks into the school year. I was just so eager to jump right into the curriculum, and now they have already developed bad habits. I don't know if I can break them."

"It's true," replied Kris, "that it's best to establish your expectations from the very beginning, but we're not too far in yet. We can still turn this around. We just need to start by defining some class expectations. So, let me ask you, what do you expect of your students?"

"I'd like them to behave well."

"Okay, what does 'behave well' mean?"

"To act as they should, I guess."

"So, how should they act?"

Sheri filled her lungs with a hint of exasperation. "I don't know; act with respect?"

"Good! We're making progress now. So, is it safe to say that you have a class expectation to treat the students and teacher with respect?"

"Well, sure, I suppose so. Let's make that an expectation." Then realizing her minor success, Sheri burst with excitement. "Oh my! Look at me! I have an expectation! I'm making popcorn! I…"

Kris interrupted, sensing a new monologue approaching. "Sheri, your pot's still in the cupboard. We're just getting started."

"Oh."

"But a hidden pot won't do us much good," Kris continued, "so let's see how we can reach in and pull it out." In preparation for the oncoming lesson, the two sat a little taller in their white, leather chairs.

"We now need to put some definition to it. Respect is a good expectation because it is a general ideal that encompasses many specific behaviors, and it can be individually applied. However, its abstract nature makes it difficult for students to understand exactly what you mean. So, this *expectation* needs to be further defined with concrete *standards*. Standards are the specific minimums to which all students must conform for a given expectation."

"Alright, how do I do that?"

"A standard usually begins with a concrete action verb and is expressed in positive terms. To define standards, I've found it helps to ask the question, 'What does following this expectation look like?' I'll give you an example. If you had an expectation to 'demonstrate responsibility,' that might look like students, among other things, completing all their work and arriving to class on time."

"'Complete all your work' and 'arrive on time,'" Sheri repeated. "I see how these add some definition to the expectation."

"Exactly. They would be hard for a student to misinterpret. Plus, they're stated in positive terms. Statements like 'no late work' or 'no tardies' can feel restrictive and demeaning, but these are enabling and empowering. And though they basically say the same thing, the change in semantics can make a big difference for a student."

Sheri's face lit up with understanding. "Yes! I see! Okay now, I want to try with my first expectation. I need some standards for 'respect.'"

"Great. So, what does 'respect' look like?"

Sheri sat back and mulled over the question. "Respect. I suppose it looks like many things." Her brow furrowed as her mind searched for the right standard. "Okay, I think I've got one. No chewing gum."

Kris smiled at the valiant effort. "Well now, that's a start. It is specific and defined. Yet it sounds a little more like a rule than a standard because it's stated in negative terms. How about, 'save gum for home?'"

"Oh good, I like that better," Sheri agreed. "And I've got another one too. What do you think about, 'no spit wads?'"

Kris raised an eyebrow in redirection.

"Oh yeah, positive. Uh, maybe, 'save saliva for one's self.'"

Kris burst into laughter, completely unable to maintain her composure. Sheri chuckled too, for she understood that Kris's reaction was not meant to belittle. Perhaps that last standard really was a bit of a stretch.

"Let's take a step back," Kris interjected, still struggling to keep a straight face. "Your gum and saliva standards do fit the definition, but they seem a tad on the fringes of the expectation of respect. Would you agree?"

After Sheri's nod of agreement, Kris continued.

"I suppose if gum and spit wads were a major problem, these standards would be perfect. However, let's look at what your students really seem to need. Let's target that which would be most influential in creating the classroom environment you're seeking."

"Good point," Sheri responded. "Well, you've seen my class. The bottom line seems to be that they talk out of turn and are always off task."

"So how can you address those breaches of your expectation with specific standards? Remember to begin with a concrete action verb and use positive terms."

The wheels in Sheri's head raced forward until they caught hold of the perfect standards. "Got it! 'Raise your hand to speak' and 'focus on the appropriate task.'"

Desperately needing approval, Sheri held her breath while waiting for Kris's response. Yet whether for effect or sheer personal amusement, Kris withheld her reaction for an extended moment. The tension within Sheri stretched like a rubber band, and if Kris didn't respond soon, she'd just might have snapped.

Eventually, Kris released a hint of a smile, which was all Sheri needed. She jumped to her feet and clapped her hands in celebration.

"I did it! Those standards are just perfect! This is great! I can't believe I…"

"…Sheri," Kris interrupted with a hearty grin, "you've done well. This is a good start."

"Oh Kris, thank you! Without you I could have never done this. I was doing so poorly and failing my students so miserably that I…"

"…Oh no, Sheri. Let me affirm a concrete standard for here in the Counselor Corner; it is to 'always tell the truth.' With your passion and motivation, you weren't failing anybody. You just needed a little course correction. You're now beginning to see how expectations and standards create the necessary boundaries for your students to learn and grow. With a little more effort, they will know exactly what is expected of them, both behaviorally and academically, and you'll keep developing into that influential teacher you've dreamed of becoming."

Sheri breathed deeply to calm her anxiety. Today was the day she'd toss the kernels in a pot, but now as the beginning of class approached, her nerves threatened her composure. What if they pushed back? What if they didn't listen? Sheri knew what to do, but now doubted that doing so would do any good. What if the lid burst off and her plans maliciously backfired?

The warning bell rang for first period and students streamed into the room. They clumped together in unified clusters, committed to their conversations as if that was the very purpose of class, for in reality, until that point, it had been.

"Good morning, class." The ritual began with her usual kind request and accompanying student snub.

"Excuse me, students. Could we begin, please?" True to habit, they ignored her second, more forceful appeal.

"Hey! Quiet down!" And the routine culminated in Sheri's high-pitched screech.

"Thank you. Now, we're going to start class a little differently today. Let's step away from our persuasive speeches for a few minutes," to which the students erupted with cheers, "and have a little chat about a key word," which was met by a collective groan. Sheri chose to temporarily ignore the very behavior that she was about to address.

"Please tell me, what do you think of when you hear the word 'respect?'"

A boy shouted from the middle of the pack, "Something my parents don't give me!"

"You mean, something you never give us girls," retorted a sassy voice from the back.

Uproar ensued. A deafening mixture of laughter and banter swirled and swelled until Sheri could do nothing but yell over the top to restore temporary order.

"I apologize," Sheri continued once the noise settled. "Let me rephrase the question. How can we show respect for each other in class?"

The students looked around the room in silence, unable to think of any viable answer. Eventually, one student near the front nervously raised her hand. Once called on, she related, "Perhaps we could start by not yelling at each other."

Sheri felt pleased at the honest answer. Hoping to milk the moment, she followed up with the same student, "Very good. Now, how would speaking kindly to each other help us learn?"

Another boy seated near the first blurted out, "Maybe then we could actually hear you!"

> From 1.2.1 –
> "Introducing expectations, standards, and procedures can be done quickly, within the flow of instructions."

Sheri ignored the sarcasm and replied with an endearing giggle peculiar to that species of teacher who is fully in it for their students. "Now wouldn't that be nice? Any other ideas?"

She was met by another round of silence as the students digested this unordinary conversation. Eventually, a different student raised his hand and offered, "It could help us focus better on writing and stuff."

"Perfect! What fabulous students you are! That is exactly what I'm hoping to create. We want to make this class more exciting and worthwhile by learning in an environment of respect."

Sheri walked over to the board and wrote the word "respect" in big, bold letters. She then drew two lines extending outward from her written expectation and turned back to her students.

"There are many ways to show respect in class, but I'd like us to first focus on two basic standards." Sheri raised her hand to the board to write as she spoke. "First, you must 'raise your hand to speak.' Second, you must 'focus on the appropriate task.' Following these standards will…"

> From 1.2.1 –
> "Communicate [expectations] in plain terms through modeling, discussion, and practice."

As the brief discussion continued followed by the day's lesson, Sheri felt thrilled at her students' positive response. They had listened; they had understood. Despite Sheri's initial doubts, the class had willingly conformed to her expectation, which left her bursting with inner excitement.

And yet, her inexperience blinded Sheri to the challenges that still remained. Yes, she'd had a good day, but yes, it was bound to be tested.

"…And then, we discussed specific examples of what it means to show respect. It was incredible! I'm telling you, Kris is a genius! My students were awesome the rest of class. Kris pretty much solved our whole problem with a snap of her fingers. She just gave me a pot-full of popcorn…"

Mr. Alex Clemmington, history teacher and assistant football coach, did his best to survive the verbal blasting from this overly animated newbie. Her words flew at him faster than an all-pro defensive back, and he was left alone to dodge each shout of enthusiasm, praise of Kris, and awkward reference to popcorn. He only managed the occasional "yeah" and "uh-huh" between her rare pauses for breath.

But that didn't stop Paul.

"Bravo kid," he blurted. "Now the real trick is to make those urchins do the same tomorrow. Harder than it seems. Good luck with that pile of bowling balls."

Sheri jolted back in her chair as if physically struck. Somewhat deflated yet retaining hope, she inquired as to what Paul meant.

"Well kid, you'll soon find that these tweens, due to some awful twist of evolution, daily revert back to some sort of inferior, pubescent primate. Long arms to poke you, big mouth to talk back, and a primeval drive to zero in on nothing but the neighboring lass with a pink bow glued to the side of her head. Success with this breed is fleeting. Now, if you ask me…"

"…I don't believe anyone ever asked you."

Trisha's unmistakable haughty voice interrupted Paul as she gracefully glided from the fridge to the crushed ice machine. Her pitch black hair was pulled back in her traditional tight bun while her pointed nose aimed downward toward all those beneath.

"Well, good afternoon to you too, little Ms. Teacher-of-the-Decade. How's our Trish doing today?"

"Just teacher of the year, Paul – three years running that is," Trisha replied while crunching on her ice for emphasis. She then turned her attention to Sheri. "Don't mind him. Paul prefers counting down to June's retirement and year-round bowling to actually teaching students."

"Amen! First frame's almost over, Trish!"

Trisha turned to fully face Sheri, leaving her back to do the responding to Paul. "The name's Trisha LaValle. (Crunch) Eighth grade mathematics, the high classes, geometry and algebra 2 mainly, seeing as how I get the top scores in the district each year. Now, if you want those students to behave, you've got to whip them into shape. That's how I've done it for years, and I believe my track record speaks for itself. No nonsense. No talking. No wasted time. (Crunch)"

As Trisha's advice trailed off, Sheri's confusion grew. Kris had taught her one thing which Paul had discredited. Trisha was teaching another which contradicted Kris. She was new and impressionable, and all these differing methodologies did nothing but perplex her.

> From 2.2.2 – "Efforts to be professional should not result in a stiff, business-like approach."

"Just don't take their garbage, and you'll be fine. (Crunch)"

Class the next day had begun as the previous had concluded. Despite Sheri's worries, her students had thus far behaved surprisingly well. She now felt able to focus on teaching the content, which was a refreshing change of pace.

"So students, who can raise their hand and tell us if this fast food radio ad primarily uses ethos, pathos, or logos to persuade us to eat at their restaurant?"

Sheri called on one of the several students who had raised their hand. "Ethos."

"Good. Now, tell me why."

She called on another. "Well uh, they, like, keep talking about how long they've been in business and how they're so popular and stuff."

"Exactly! Well done! Now, did anyone happen to notice any logos?"

Many hands shot up. Sheri's heart did the same at her students' active participation. They were actually listening and participating! It was all she could do to keep her feet from lifting off the floor in celebration.

This time before she could call on one of the many compliant hands, a boy blurted out, "Value menu, baby! Why pay three bucks for some chicken nuggets while these guys'll give 'em to ya for half?"

"Great answer!" Sheri responded. "You found how they're enticing you with logic."

> From 1.3.1 – "Always follow through on [expectations], standards, and procedures."

Sheri, in her enthusiasm, didn't notice all the rest of the hands dejectedly drop when she accepted the answer of he who didn't follow the class standard.

She continued. "So, what about pathos? Did anyone notice any of that?"

Only a few hands raised this time, while a couple other students shouted, "No!"

The discussion began to lag somewhat as Sheri's ears picked up on some hushed whispering between a couple of girls off to the side. Yet still, she pressed on.

"Really? No pathos? What is pathos again?"

Two other brewing conversations began. Backpedaling, Sheri caught the eye of one of the girls from the first conversation and dished out her best "stop-it" glare as a couple students voiced an answer to the question without raising their hands. The few students with their hands in the air put them down, one of whom looked over at his neighbor and whispered something that made the other giggle. A low hum of voices continued to grow until it swelled into a persistent rumble. Sheri again glared at the group of girls off to the side, but by that time there were several other conversations popping up around the room.

"Hands please! Remember our standard to raise your hand if you wish to speak." Sheri's feeble attempt to restore order brought the rumble back down to a temporary hum; however, it was only a twig holding back the dam – it could only contain the river for so long.

"Thank you. Okay now, pathos. Who can give us an example of how this restaurant could have used pathos, or an appeal to emotion, in their advertisement?"

A student blurted out, "Start crying! Tears sell burgers, right?" The class erupted into a roar of laughter.

Choking back tears herself, Sheri's mind swirled and her heart dipped. How had their positive momentum changed so quickly? What happened to her once studious scholars? Their behavior had transformed so fast that she couldn't tell why, nor could she slow their downward spiral. What happened?

Sheri kept her composure just long enough to hand out a worksheet. The students received it to only half work and half talk with friends. As the noise increased, Paul's voice rang even louder in Sheri's mind, fully drowning out the memory of all of Kris's once promising lessons. She concluded that Paul was right, and despite her best efforts, she had failed once again.

With the dam now collapsed and the waters raging forth, the students carried on for the remainder of class. Upon the sound of the dismissal bell, the flood poured out the door, leaving Sheri alone, feeling buried beneath the weight of her collapsed expectations.

—∞—

If there had been a fly on the wall in Kris's office that afternoon, it would have observed quite a spectacle. Sheri's emotional outbreak grew like a child on a swing. She swung back with sorrow, forth with anger, back with denial, then forth with despair. The stir of the ride produced anything but pleasure. The perpetual back and forth brought vertigo, fatigue, and nausea, and all Kris could do was endure.

After a half box of tissues and the remainder of Kris's chocolate, Sheri collapsed into the soft, white chair, nestling into its safety as if it were the padded walls of an asylum. Now that Sheri appeared completely drained, Kris finally felt it safe to proceed.

"I'm sorry for your poor experience, Sheri. These things take time, and you're only a couple of days into changing your classroom culture. Come on, let me ask a few questions to see what lessons we can learn from this."

The only response Sheri was able to muster was a childish shoulder shrug. Kris stretched that into a green light.

"Now, I believe I understand how class ended, but can you tell me how it began?"

Sheri's head fell into her open palms, still recovering from her eruption. "That's the worst part," she bemoaned. "It actually started quite well."

"What could be bad about that?"

"Because I ruined it! They were great, and I don't know how, but somehow I completely ruined it!"

"Okay, I hear you. Why don't you tell me about the beginning of class?"

Sheri sat up slightly and began to summarize. She explained how they had started class by briefly discussing the expectations and standards they had implemented the previous day. They then got right to the day's lesson, and the students responded very well. They raised their hands, they listened, they eagerly participated – it was all she could have hoped for. And then all of a sudden, without warning, they exploded! It seemed to happen so fast. They changed from angels to demons before she could blink.

> From 1.2.2 – "Regularly take time to review [expectations]. This is a preventative measure to solidifies the concepts in long term memory."

"Hold on," interrupted Kris. "I already know about the explosion, so let's rewind a bit. Now think, Sheri. What happened? What triggered their change in behavior? Tell me about your lesson."

Sheri explained their discussion on persuasion and its application to advertising. She elaborated on how she'd ask questions and then call on students with their hands raised for a response.

As she continued, Kris's face broke into a knowing smile. "At any point did a student yell out an answer without raising a hand?"

"Hello!" burst Sheri with a sarcastic twang. "Haven't you been listening? They yelled for like half an hour straight!"

"Yes, I understand that," replied Kris even-toned, "but I can see where this is going as I've seen it all too often before. When striving to establish clear expectations and standards, there will come a point in most lessons where you'll hit a crossroads. There is often a turning point where your boundaries will be challenged, and you will stand at the crossroads, faced with the decision on whether or not to follow through. In this case, there must have been a first time when a student called out and challenged your standard."

Sheri, listening intently, nodded with understanding. Kris continued, "So let me ask you, that first time a student called out, did you acknowledge the answ…"

"No!" Sheri interrupted defensively. "That's the class standard!"

However, her continued response began to slow as she recalled the details of what happened. "I would never…" her voice softened, "break…" her eyes dropped, "my own…" Kris smiled, "expectations," she trailed off to a whisper. Kris let the uneasy pause continue for as long as it took Sheri to come to the right conclusion on her own.

Eventually, Sheri proceeded pensively. "It was me, wasn't it? I think I see my fault. I didn't follow through, not even on my own expectation. And once they saw it, they knew they didn't have to follow it either."

> From 1.3.1 – "Breaking your own standard [will reinforce] the very behavior you're trying to prevent."

Kris smiled with empathy. "Following through on your expectations is more challenging than it seems. It's more important than it seems too."

"But Kris, tell me, is it that big of a deal for a student to call out a correct answer? They were participating and on task. They were learning."

"No, it's not that big of a deal," replied Kris, "that is, if it weren't an expectation. Once you've established the boundaries, you must follow through. Otherwise, the students will push against their softening limits, often breaking right through. If there is a time you want the standard to be broken, like being able to speak without raising a hand during a group discussion, then specifically tell the students the beginning *and ending* of the allowable breach of your standard. But in all other instances, you must constantly reinforce the walls by following through on all expectations and standards. Doing so will strengthen the class environment, providing fertile ground for learning to occur."

Sheri sat back and considered the concept. Yes, she had both defined and communicated her expectations, but all "talk" with no "do" hadn't cut it. She hadn't walked her talk, so the students just, well, talked.

"So, how can I best follow through?" asked Sheri.

As the conversation continued, Sheri hopped back on her emotional swing. Except this time each pump of her legs brought increasingly higher feelings of hope, knowledge, and confidence.

Sheri arrived at school the next morning to find a half sheet of paper on her desk. As yesterday afternoon's conversation at the Counselor Corner had continued, Kris introduced Sheri to a valuable exercise that Kris herself had practiced as a teacher for years: reflective journal writing. Kris had explained how journaling is a great way to reflect on past performance for the purpose of shaping the future through synthesizing thoughts and experiences.

Plus, a little reflective writing would be a great way for Sheri to de-stress – an obvious need.

At first, Sheri felt quite apprehensive. She was scared that reflecting on the failures of the past two weeks would do nothing but perpetuate her downward spiral. So instead, Kris had committed to create a list of guiding questions to assist in her first attempt, and Sheri had committed to being succinct, a personal challenge to be sure.

Journal Entry – September 7

What have I done well? *Despite my several failures, I'm totally dedicated to these kids. I really do love them. It's that passion that drives me to prepare hard and teach with enthusiasm. I want them to succeed so badly that I'm willing to do whatever it takes to help them, even if it means changing my own bad habits (or writing a journal!).*

> From 2.2.1 – "Teachers should approach their position at an even high standard than they expect of their students."

What do I need to most improve? *Only one? Really? Okay, I'll say raising expectations. They must be clear, challenging, and reinforced with consistent follow-through. Until this point, they've been vague, soft, and only reinforced intermittently. Ouch!*

How should I communicate expectations? *I already introduced them in plain, explicit terms. Now we need to review and practice them in quick discussions for the next week or so. We'll then review them periodically throughout the year as a positive reminder, assessing how we're doing and celebrating our success. (We'll be successful, right?)*

> From 1.2.2 – "This process, over time, causes *your* expectations of *them* to become *their* expectations of themselves."

Why must I / how can I follow through on expectations? *The "why" is pretty simple – just look at the last two weeks! If I don't follow our expectations, how can I expect my students to? I must follow through so they clearly understand* the boundaries. How? I can recognize appropriate behavior, like thanking students for raising their hands. If talking out of turn, I could use proximity, give quiet reminders with voice or gestures, redo a noisy transition, or simply not move forward until all are with me.

How can quick pacing help maintain high expectations? I've always been taught that "Idle hands are the devil's workshop," (thanks Mom!). If I pick up the pace of instruction and transitions, they won't even have time to goof around. So, increasing my academic expectations should have a beneficial by-product.

> From 4.1 – "The first three principles prepare the way for teachers to do what they do best – teach."

What do I want the rest of the school year to look like? How I always dreamed it would be! A fun, energetic environment where students are engaged and working to achieve their best. I don't want poor behavior and low motivation to slow our learning. I want to create an environment where each student is able to focus on academic achievement, where their success becomes our reality. Ah! Do you think we can really do it?

Boisterous and unruly, students filed in the next day in the manner they had become accustomed – loud. Yet today, it didn't take long for students to notice a sheet of pastel-green paper sitting atop each desk. The newness of the scene peaked their curiosity, so they dislodged themselves from their conversations to find their seats and read the bold lettering at the top.

"You have exactly three minutes to complete the grammar assignment below. Good luck!"

Shocked, the students glanced around at their peers, a little doubtful that such a change in expectations could be for real. With furrowed brows and rolling eyes, they looked up at their teacher as the tardy bell sounded. Sheri didn't say a word. She just smiled, raised a hand-held timer, and clicked start.

A wave of energy rippled throughout the room as students anxiously searched for their pencils and began hastily working on the assignment, their opportunity for full completion diminishing with each passing second. Sheri walked around to the delightful tune of scribbling pencils and whispered words of encouragement along the way.

With a minute and a half elapsed, a pair of late-comers clamored in with their traditional gusto; yet, the drastic change to the newly-placed energy of their classmates stopped them dead in their tracks. The duo looked around to make sure they were in the right class, which led them to meet the eyes of their teacher. She greeted them with a smile and silently mouthed while pointing to their desks, "only one minute left." The pair looked at each other and then scurried to their seats.

"Time's up," Sheri told the class at the beep of the timer. "Please put down your pencils and turn over your papers."

While most complied, Sheri spotted a boy near the front still vigorously writing. With Kris's lessons urging her forward, Sheri stepped toward the student, discretely snatched up the paper, and continued on as if nothing ever happened.

> From 1.3.1 – "Quick transitions and lesson pacing avoid lag time where breaches in standards and procedures are more likely to occur."

"Thank you, students, for coming in so quickly and getting right to work. That was a wonderful way to begin. Now, please quietly hand your papers up to the front and take out your writing journals."

With this request, the students burst into their customary chatter while casually handing up their assignments. It was like the air being let out of a tightly stretched balloon; they deflated from their previous taut and rigid state to again become relaxed, talkative, and flat.

> From 3.4 – "Recognize desired behavior."

"Excuse me," Sheri interrupted with a pleasant ring to her voice. "Could you please hand the papers back to their owners? Thank you. Now, who can remind us how I asked you to hand in your assignments?"

As the papers found their way back, the students were surprised into silence. After a few elongated, awkward moments while Sheri patiently waited, one girl sheepishly called out, "Quietly?"

She was ignored. Sheri continued to look about the room with an expectant grin as if no one had said a thing. The class didn't seem to understand why Sheri hadn't acknowledged the answer, so she offered a friendly reminder of the standard by raising her own hand as a model.

With a silent, echoing "oh," several students raised their hand, including the girl who originally called out, on whom Sheri called again.

"Quietly," she again stated, yet with a little more confidence.

"Exactly!" Sheri responded. "Thanks for reminding us. Okay now, let's give it another shot." And this time the students obeyed to perfection.

"Well done, guys. I appreciate your quick work. Now let's get right to the day's activity."

Sheri could barely contain her excitement. Her mind wrapped around the image of a large bowl overflowing with fistfuls of fluffy, white popcorn. Yeah sure, she might have been getting ahead of herself, but Sheri had always been one to indulge in a dream.

The sound of a whispering pair of students near the back of the room woke Sheri from her reverie. Somewhat troubled but retaining hope, she resisted the urge to shush them. Instead, she gathered her wits and slowly strolled toward the whisperers while continuing on with the instructions.

"The last few days we've enjoyed learning the art of persuasion. Now, let me remind you that the ultimate goal of this unit is to write a hypothetical speech to Mr. Phippen, persuading him to change a particular aspect of the school."

Sheri had reached the pair by the time she finished the statement. Without ever even talking to or looking at the chatty duo, they halted their conversation, fully understanding their teacher's wishes simply by her proximity.

"And today is an important day," Sheri related as she moved back to the front of the room, hoping to retain the positive momentum. "Today we're going to brainstorm and select topics for our speeches!"

"Soda machine!" one boy blurted from habit.

"No homework!" shouted another.

"No girls!" This elicited an eruption of male laughter accompanied by feigned outrage from some howling females.

Sheri bit down on her bottom lip. Her natural inclination was to yell for quiet, but she had committed herself to follow her own expectation of respect. So, she calmly and quickly reflected on an appropriate course of action, knowing full well that this was a pivotal moment in defining expectations to strengthen their classroom culture. This was it. This was their crossroads of the day.

As the class stormed on, Sheri calmly stepped over to a bulletin board hanging just off to the side. There, tacked to the bottom corner, was a half-sized manila envelope, so plain and inconspicuous that the few students who detected her movement couldn't tell whether it was new or had simply never been noticed. Sheri reached in and pulled out three quarter-sheet laminated red cards.

A few more detected her surprising under-reaction, which spurred on a small reduction to the collective clamor. Continuing to resist hollering over the noise, Sheri swiftly moved to the desks of the three students who had breached the class standards by blurting out. This unexpected action caught everyone's attention, so that by the time she had distributed the cards and returned to the front of the room, the class had fallen silent.

> From 1.3.1 – "The particular method used [to follow through] is not nearly as important as the fact that you use it consistently, following through with regularity."

"Students, I love how quickly you quieted down. And I love even more how many of you remembered our class standards of raising your hand to speak and focusing on the appropriate task. Following these standards really helps us enjoy our activities and learning. I can tell that soon our entire class will remember to follow these standards."

The three students with red cards looked down to discover their purpose.

> From 1.3.1 – "Be quick when addressing [breaches]. Elongated lectures produce the opposite of the desired effect. Preplan strategies."

"Admissions Ticket. You may be admitted to the hall at the end of class only after having presented Ms. Price with your ticket."

The three looked up at Ms. Price in disbelief, but she had already continued on with the lesson.

Sheri floated through the door to the teachers' lounge, smiling and dreamy eyed. She glided to the fridge, grabbed her carrot sticks and string cheese, and continued her one-woman parade to a back table, completely oblivious to the presence of her colleagues who were curiously staring at her unusual demeanor.

Paul, as one would expect, was the first to break the silence. "Hey twinkle toes, you find your prince?"

Yet Sheri had settled in comfortably, alone upon of a black, plastic chair at a table along the back wall. Though the lounge was windowless, she was completely lost in her thoughts while soaking in the amorous rays of some imaginary sunshine.

Journal Entry – September 23

Kris keeps reminding me to reflect in my journal, and while I really needed those reminders at first, now it's become an old habit – either that or needed therapy!

Our last few meetings have been quite different than the first where I was a blubbering basket case. And maybe it's the disparity between the two that makes it feel so good to celebrate together all the positive changes she's helped me make. She seems just as happy for me and my students as I am. She even told me how one student in their last counseling session mentioned how much she enjoys my class. Wow!

The most surprising thing to me about this culture shifting is how long it takes. Whenever I think our expectations are fully implemented, they forget. We then kindly review them together, which brings us right back to where we want to be – before they go and break them again. Yet, I take comfort in seeing how the intervals between breaches are becoming farther and farther apart. Kris says that a class culture is seldom completely devoid of such disturbances, but with time and consistency they will become the rare exception.

> From 1.2.2 –
> "Throughout the duration of the year, occasionally discuss the purpose of expectations, standards, and procedures as a source of reflection and application."

Now, I've found that the most rewarding aspect of this isn't that I don't have to yell to get attention anymore (although that's certainly a plus!), but it's how much we're able to accomplish in class. Since students are talking to each other less, and our pacing has picked up, we are able to do and learn so much more. It's great!

Also, sometimes I feel I should relax a little and back off on the follow-through now that they may be able to handle it, but Kris tells me to stick with it. It takes a lot longer than a couple of weeks to change habits and create a culture. And yet sometimes I still forget to follow through, even without meaning to, but the students and I try to be patient as we both work on forming new habits.

Okay, so this afternoon Kris taught me what she thinks is the next step I need to implement – class procedures. As always, she gave me an assignment. Now, we've already talked a fair amount about procedures, so she just generated some review questions based on our discussions. See below.

What is a class procedure? *A specific process students follow to accomplish a task, like how to enter the room or hand in papers.*

Why should I use class procedures? *Procedures help with the flow and operations of the class, both quickening the pace and minimizing disruptions. My students should feel safer in a predictable environment, where they know how to act in common situations. Also, they will be empowered by understanding their boundaries and how they can act freely within them. Plus, I'll avoid the frustration of interruptions, noisy transitions, and repeating myself excessively. Hurray!*

How do I implement a class procedure? *Explicitly. Students won't learn what you want them to do through osmosis, hoping they'll magically figure it out on their own. Use three steps: First, clearly communicate when to use the procedure and its specific steps. Second, assess their understanding. Third, practice and reinforce until it becomes a habit.*

What are some examples of possible class procedures? *How to enter the room, sharpen a pencil, turn in homework, pass in papers, pass back papers, turn off lights, ask a question, get absent work, be productive when finished early, get classroom materials (dictionary, textbook, etc.), tell the teacher you need a tissue or go to the restroom, leave class, etc.*

Upon reflection, my transitions now are still a little loud and slow. And I never thought of it before, but it does bug me when we're in the middle of a lesson and a student blurts out that they need a tissue. Talk about a momentum killer! If I can train them to just give me a sign, it would solve the problem. I'm sure there are plenty more procedures I could use that would similarly help.

The scene in the teachers' lounge that late fall afternoon was like a collage of individually distinct hues, all unified to a single purpose – student success. It was easy to observe Kris's influence weaving throughout the portrait with each stroke striving to apply universal principles to their individual situations and according to their unique styles and strengths. Some splotches of the collage shined in bold red, where self-interest was sacrificed to prepare safe yet engaging learning environments. Other sections glimmered in cool ocean green, wise with years of experience. These were contrasted by other radiant shades, including a single vivid yellow, new and excited yet naïve with inexperience.

But in this collage, there was a lone pocket of gray lurking around the fringes. Paul sat himself near the back of the image, away from the lounge door as if repulsed by the thought of stepping back through it. He used to enjoy the spotlight of center stage, but as the primary colors displayed by his colleagues strengthened with the help of Counselor Kris, his dulling influence had weakened. Now only able to draw in another miserable friend or two, Paul reveled in his darkened corner in either stubborn silence or antagonistic grumbling.

Today, Paul grumbled. He grumbled loudly to the few he'd managed to drag down to accompany his misery. Though others tried to ignore him, he endlessly droned on from topic to topic: from his ignorant students to the reproachful school administration, from the glory of last weekend's bowling tournament to the wonder of his approaching retirement. He was only slowed by his occasional slurp from the 64 ounce cola he'd purchased at the neighboring gas station.

> <u>From 4.2.2</u> – The ultimate goal of "self-centered instruction [is] fulfilling one's own needs at the possible expense of students."

This dark disturbance briefly floundered upon the entrance of Mr. Phippen. However, as the gangly assistant principal peered into the fridge in search of his small Tupperware filled with remnants of the previous night's dinner, Paul recalled the administrator's harmless nature. Regaining his poise and reveling in his miserable mood, Paul whispered some juvenile quips to his comrades. He targeted the corny part in Mr. Phippen's hair and the supposed trauma the toothpick's belly button must be enduring from the awkwardly too-far-north placement of his belt. "Watch out!" Paul joked. "It might start fighting back at any moment!"

Like a group of snickering eighth grade boys, the trio erupted in immature laughter. Upon settling down, Paul muttered one last jab as the unsuspecting assistant principal strode passed. "Oh, pardon me, it must be an inny."

Mr. Phippen found his way from the fridge to the bright yellow corner of the collage, adjacent along the back wall of the darkening thundercloud to the south. Lunch in hand, he sat down at an almost empty table. The only other occupant was Sheri, quietly reading from a thick young adult fantasy novel. The presence of the unexpected company awoke Sheri from her indulgent tranquility not known just weeks before – before she traversed her teaching crossroads with Kris's aid. She put down her book and smiled at Mr. Phippen, a little surprised at his presence in the lounge.

"Ms. Price... uh, Sheri. How's your book... uh, novel? Enjoying a little quiet before fifth period?"

"Why Mr. Phippen! How nice to see you," Sheri exclaimed. "And yes, I needed a little breather after the busy day we've had so far. My third period eighth graders, in particular, delivered some rousing persuasive speeches. I am just so proud of those kids! I had some students that did better than I even thought possible. Hand gestures, props, involving the audience. I even had one student break out in song! The class loved it! I'm just so pleased with how well they're doing. At the beginning of the year we really struggled, but now! Oh my! ..."

Sheri's animated speech of her own was cut short by a burst of laughter from the shady direction of Paul and company.

After the interruption died down, Mr. Phippen continued. "Sounds wonderful. I'm glad to hear of the improvement. So... uh, what happened to turn things around?"

"Kris!" Sheri exclaimed. "It was all Kris. I was dying. I couldn't keep the students under control. She taught me about creating a classroom culture of success, setting high expectations, and saved my life! I still have a lot of work to do, but my students are so much better after implementing her suggestions."

"Kris, our... uh, new school counselor?"

"That's right! She's amazing! I don't know what I would have done without her! And you know what? I think you should also stop by my class sometime to observe and give me some feedback. I'm always looking to improve; these kids deserve it. And that's one of the things Kris taught me. As good as these students are, they come to us with the ability to choose. We can't make their choices for them, but we can create a classroom culture most conducive to them making the right choices themselves. And another thing..."

> From 4.2.3 – "Student centered [teachers] are willing learners."

Mr. Phippen, along with several other nearby teachers, grinned at Sheri's enthusiasm. As her speech stretched on, many took note of the consistency of her passion. Her brightening yellow shimmer, similar to the rising sun, seemed to enhance the other color of the collage, bringing life and beauty to all within her influence.

In the early morning, well before the beginning of school, Sheri sat at her classroom desk taking a moment to gaze out the window and enjoy the serenity of the bright white flakes of the first December snowfall. Temporarily entranced by the mesmerizing swirl of the gentle silver flecks, Sheri indulged in the memory of the journey of her first few months as a teacher.

Sheri snickered at her initial naïve enthusiasm. For years she had created in her mind a utopian-like teacher dream land. Perfect students. Engaging lessons. Laughing. Loving. Learning.

Yet, oh, how her euphoric vision had been racked across the coals by the flippant attitudes of youth! Chatty mouths. Sealed ears. Confusion. Chaos. Crying!

Their once untoward behavior flared in stark contrast to the peaceful winter scene before her. However, both she and her students had come a long way in just a few months' time. Things had finally begun to change once she understood and committed to creating a class environment most conducive to success. She began spending as much time preparing culture interventions as lesson plans. She began explicitly teaching expectations. She began to consistently follow through and hold students accountable.

Over time, Sheri had noticed a shift in her students. She at first had to be vigilant to an extreme, following through and reinforcing her expectations by the minute. But now, she realized her students needed less intervention. Her expectations, standards, and procedures had become habitual, natural even. With time, they had actually become the culture of her class.

> From 1.1.1 – "When in doubt [in defining expectations], err on the high side; students can perform at a much higher level than are often given credit."

This shift allowed them to focus on what really mattered, learning and success. All the time and effort initially used to create such a culture had already doubled in return. It was like the prewriting of a persuasive speech. If a person jumped right into the speech without any preparation, they'd likely fall flat. Yet when taking the time upfront to outline arguments, anticipate counterarguments, and draft impactful punch lines, the real speech is transformed into an eloquent masterpiece.

And it was just December! Sheri would be able to maximize several more months of valuable time devoid of the persistent rainfall of their past. It is worth it!

"Good morning, Ms. Price." Sheri, awoke from her contemplation and turned around to see Kris standing in the doorway on the other side of the room, smiling and leaning against the frame.

"Well there, good morning to you, Kris. To what do I owe such a pleasant visit this morning?"

"Oh, to learn from the master," Kris playfully quipped.

"Hey now!" retorted Sheri, devaluing the compliment with a teasing tone. "Save your role reversal for Mrs. Argyle's theatre class."

Kris chuckled in response, "Actually, I'm here to observe another student who's been struggling in a few classes."

"Are you sure you're not here to save these kids from all my mistakes?"

"Oh, come on now. You know as well as I how great you're doing. These kids adore you."

Their conversation was interrupted by the entrance of a group of girls, still a couple of minutes before the ring of the warning bell. Upon wrapping up their pleasantries, Kris found a seat near the back corner while Sheri placed a stack of half sheet pastel-green papers on a music stand next to the door. As students began to quietly file in, Kris observed how upon entering each student picked up a paper, grabbed their language arts journal from a nearby crate, sat at their desks, and began diligently working. By the time the warning bell rang, nearly every seat was filled with working students while the hallway still echoed with noise. It was as if they preferred the culture of the class to the dynamics of the hall.

Kris noted how many students had even completed the warm-up by the time the late bell rang, and then automatically took out something productive to do while awaiting their teacher's instructions. Some studied their journals for an upcoming grammar quiz. Others revised their draft personal narratives. Some simply took out a novel and silently read.

> From 1.1.2 –
> "Procedures… simplify and quicken the pace of class."

All this occurred while Sheri moved around the room, quietly helping individual students. Her cheery step and encouraging disposition as she bounced about resembled a butterfly pollinating a classroom of blooming spring flowers, even now at the onset of winter.

Within a few minutes, most had finished. At the appropriate time, Sheri broke the studious silence with a single, small declaration.

"Pass them in."

Immediately, students dropped their task and handed their papers up the five rows of desks and sat quietly waiting for their next activity.

"Well done this morning on your grammar warm up; those I saw looked great. Now," Sheri paused for effect, "today is finally the day I promised would come throughout our whole personal narrative unit." A silent wave of excitement rushed around the room. "You've been working so hard and doing so well revising these rough drafts. So now, in preparation for completing your final draft, today is finally the day we will get in small groups to share with our peers!"

This time the silent wave became audible as several exclamations of delight escaped the mouths of the eager students.

"You'll find instructions for the activity written on the board, and I'm sure this stellar class will read and follow them precisely, as you always do. So class, are you ready to take out your drafts and begin?"

Not a student moved. They all intently stared at their teacher, eagerly waiting her signal. Sheri held the moment with an exaggerated smile.

"Go!"

As the students snatched up their drafts and grouped together, Kris beamed from the back. She observed Sheri flutter from group to group, intently listening to each excited student and leading the laughter at the punch lines.

Chapter Two Author's Note

First year teachers are a treasure to the education profession. What they lack in experience they often make up in enthusiasm. Though they come to the classroom with much still to learn, their veteran colleagues can also learn much from them.

Empowered is written with characters stereotypical to an extreme, such as an enthusiastic newbie or a burnt out long-termer, for two primary purposes: First, for ease of personal application, and second, to better demonstrate the four guiding principles of culture creating. (Plus, it's just plain fun to identify those characteristics in our own schools – or in ourselves!) Though Sheri is an extreme example of a stereotypical first year teacher, it is not only the inexperienced who can learn a lesson in high expectations. This first principle of culture creating can be universally applied according to the particulars of any given situation.

The high expectations Sheri implemented also relate to the other three guiding principles. For instance, she reinforced the positive when following through on breached expectations. She also built relationships of respect and trust by interacting with her students in a friendly, professional manner. Though Sheri's experience primarily focused on high expectations, this principle is inseparably intertwined with the others.

Sheri's use of high expectations was for the primary purpose of behavior management. The Cliff Notes section on pages 191-202 details how expectations should also be implemented for academic purposes. Ultimately, the two are just as connected as the four principles themselves. When behavior expectations are high, classes may focus on academics. When academic expectations are high, there's no time for misbehavior. One cannot fully exist without the other.

The extremities of Sheri's story may seem farfetched. It may be challenging to visualize a teacher struggling as much as she did turning things around so quickly. However, do not mistake this story for a fairytale. Not only *can* it be done, but it *is* being done in countless classrooms like yours.

Each situation evolves around different challenges, some greater than others, yet all can achieve a measure of success similar to or greater than Sheri's. It was her natural charisma combined with her implementation of culture creating principles that enabled the success.

No other group of professionals is asked to do so much, for so many, with so little, in such a short period of time. The nation's teachers are, as a whole, commendable beyond measure. The challenges we face and the importance of our cause necessitate teachers like Sheri – passionate, diligent, flexible, and willing to learn. There is no substitute for a quality teacher. No innovative technology and no fancy educational fad can replace the influence of a wise and dedicated educator. For when a teacher's heart is properly placed and aligned with sound methodologies, he or she possesses the ability to not only change the culture of their classrooms, but also the culture of their students' lives.

Questions to Consider – Your Journal Entry #1

1. *What expectations, standards and/or procedures do I currently implement with my students? What benefits have I seen from them?*

2. *What is one expectation and/or standard that I would like to newly implement? Why would this be beneficial?*

3. *What are some unique characteristics of my class situation? What is one thing I can do to strengthen my current classroom expectations according to my unique circumstances?*

Chapter Three

Alex and the Principle of Relationships of Respect and Trust

"Hey, hey! Big Ty! Welcome back man!"

"Ah, yeah… There's the Jakester. Couldn't stay out of the weight room this summer, huh?"

"Ry-aaaan, feelin' good about Friday's game? I hear their QB's got some wheels, and his arm's a cannon. Blitz it all night, dude. I'm tellin' ya man, pressure all night."

It was Monday and the first day of school. Mr. Alex Clemmington, assistant football coach turned history teacher, greeted his students at the classroom door as they entered. He dished out high fives and fist bumps all around along with some special handshakes to some boys sporting football jerseys. On the board was written, *'Welcome to 8th Grade History! Pick a seat and begin working on the 'Getting-To-Know-You' paper."*

The students were welcomed to a classroom that resembled a cross between the teachers' lounge itself and the students' own messy teenage bedrooms. There were groups of four or five desks placed in some unidentifiable order throughout the room. Wall decorations were plastered about including a

> Relationships of Respect and Trust – Teacher relationships with individual students are built on professionalism and friendliness for the purpose of building intrinsic motivation.

> From 2.2.2 – A 'friend' teacher "interacts as a peer or equal… [and] portrays oneself as cool, funny, and/or modern."

variety of maps and other historical artifact replicas combined with random sports memorabilia. Near the back corner lay what was assumed to be the teacher's desk. It was hard to tell because of all the stacks of papers strewn about. Even the computer monitor was barely visible passed the smattering of yellow sticky notes that framed it in.

In stark contrast to the disorganization of the rest of the room, on the wall above the teacher desk hung a perfectly manicured decorative shelf, neatly organized with two framed newspaper articles, yellowed with age. These were flanked by a framed photo of Mr. Clemmington as a young teenager in full football gear. Both were delicately placed inward at an ever-so-slight angle, facing the center of the shelf as if to pay tribute to the large, well-polished trophy with a golden football player on top. The plate on the bottom of the trophy boldly stated the three most important letters in the life of a self-centered athlete – M-V-P.

Students lazily filed in and grouped together in a most predictable order. The football players staked out the back, opposite Mr. Clemmington's desk. Cheerleaders claimed the seats near their football counterparts. A couple groups of ordinary looking students formed rank around the middle of the room, while still others quietly yet reluctantly found some remaining seats up front. A few stragglers stood awkwardly just inside the door, shyly wishing for the mercy of a seating chart. Yet Mr. Clemmington didn't notice them as he hung back near the football corner with some last minute high fives while the misfits assimilated themselves amongst the pack.

> From 4.2.1 – A lesson-centered teacher does "not consider the learning needs of individual students because they care more for the positive reaction of the whole."

After the initial wave of social hierarchical segregation subsided, the students halfheartedly settled into their "Getting-To-Know-You" assignment. Mr. Clemmington wandered around interacting with students, contributing to the hum of chatter. His blue jeans and Crossroads Cougars short sleeve polo projected the appearance of his laid-back persona.

After several minutes and a crescendoing volume, the coach took the hint that they had completed as much of the assignment as they intended to, so he perched himself atop a stool at the front of the room and called for attention.

"Welcome to eighth grade American History!" the coach exclaimed with half a smirk. "I'm stoked to have you guys here. We're gonna learn loads of cool stuff and have a ton of fun. Now, I'd like to tell y'all a bit 'bout me, but figured I oughta give you first crack at it. So go ahead and share a couple things from your sheets with your group."

Noise erupted. The bulk of students boisterously talked and laughed together, ignoring their assignment sheet because they were sitting next to their friends anyway. The only exception was the few shy students who magically managed to locate each other and dutifully review the assignment. The coach meandered around and joined in the laughing himself.

After several minutes, Mr. Clemmington realized he'd been lost in a conversation with a group in the back for enough time that even those following instructions had become off task. He jumped up, trotted back to his stool, and called for the class's attention.

"Sounds like we've had a good time to kick things off. I'd love to hear from a few of you. Who can tell us something fun they did this summer?"

Students' hands shot up, with several groans and grunts seeking to attract their teacher's attention – a fact he thoroughly enjoyed. His eyes naturally navigated to the back where he called on a young lady in cheerleader attire.

"A couple friends and I spent a weekend downtown. The hotel was hot, and we like lived at the mall. It was, like, totally awesome."

"Way cool! Anyone else?"

One extra-smooth football player smirked when called on. "Took my girlfriend to the lake. Wakeboarding and swimsuits… oh yeah!"

With high fives from his crew and gasps from the rest, he obtained his desired shock reaction. Mr. Clemmington didn't quite know how to handle the colorful comment, but he eventually settled for, "Oh boy. Just make sure to be to practice by three!"

After a few more students shared, Mr. Clemmington cut them off to take his turn. "Well, many of you already know me, but for those who don't, officially, my name is Mr. Alex Clemmington. Some kids call me Mr. C., others call me Alex. The boys on the team combined the two and call me Mr. X. Whatever you'd like is cool with me."

Alex, chomping on gum, stood up from his stool and continued. "I've been coaching and teaching at East Crossroads for five years now. When I was barely older than you, I went to high school just outside the metro-area where I played four years of football. We took state my senior year, and yours truly, Mr. X, was named MVP." The class turned to follow their teacher's outstretched hand gesturing to his enshrined trophy above his sloppy desk.

The students sat back to enjoy the wasted time as their teacher continued on about his hobbies, his accomplishments, and why he decided to become a coach and teacher. "I just loved my high school days with all the sports and friends, so I'm doing this now to help y'all enjoy it as much as I did. You know, I just love me a good time."

—m—

Alex anxiously searched for the lesson plan he had printed yesterday afternoon that must have been eaten up by his desk sometime the previous night. The scene looked similar to one of his teenage students scurrying about a messy bedroom to locate a lost shoe while wearing half a shirt and tripping over piles of clothes. In fact, his disorganization wasn't the only similarity Alex shared with his students. His own dress and grooming habits mirrored theirs, with hair styles and clothing fluctuating with the latest teenage fads.

> From 2.2.1 – "Ensure your classroom is neat, welcoming, and organized."

Currently, the front of his receding hairline spiked up in prickly spines, the strength and shine of which would lead one to believe he ignored the printed recommendation on the styling gel bottle to use a mere "dime-sized" dab. He predominantly wore baggy blue jeans with the occasional game day exception of athletic shorts. He employed a small rotation of varying colors of polo shirts, most of which seemed to have shrunk with his continuing consumption of electrolyte replenishing yet sugar-filled sports drinks. Yet, the one constant on which his students could count was his ever-present well-trimmed goatee, which provided a sense of stability to his changing-with-the-tides image.

Mercifully, the desk spewed out his lesson plan just before the ring of the warning bell. Students began to enter in a similar fashion as the day previous, and Alex greeted them with similar pomp as well. As the students found their seats, Alex's high fives and boisterous salutations pressed on well passed the tardy bell.

"Alright guys, let's settle down a sec," Alex eventually declared from atop his stool. "I hope y'all enjoyed your first day. I had a blast reading through your getting-to-know-you's; this class is full of characters."

Alex paused, hoping for a reaction, some sort of reciprocated excitement, but all he saw were blank stares in return. So, he swallowed hard and continued.

"Today we start learning our American history. We get to take a look at the first European explorers in our land. It's cool stuff. So, go ahead and take out your text and open up to page six."

That announcement was greeted by a round of exaggerated groans, accented by several students loudly dropping their textbooks on their desk, blasting a round of revolutionary shots in protest. The dissatisfaction dragged out the transition, until eventually all flopped their books open and stared blankly passed the small print. Doing his best to ignore the behavior, Alex read aloud the opening paragraph then asked for a volunteer to begin the next, to which the students howled in objection.

"Mr. X, this thing's too dense to understand. Can we read with a partner instead?" This ingenious suggestion turned protest to pleading as the students joined forces with calls of consent. Alex hesitated, torn between following his plan and wanting the kids to like him. And, like foxes on a wounded rabbit, sensing weakness, they pounced. The pleading grew as they saw him weigh their request.

> From 2.2.2 – A 'friend' teacher "has low expectations, [and] doesn't hold students accountable."

Eventually, Alex gave in. The class erupted in cheers that were as strong as their earlier lamentations, giving Alex a feeling of adolescent gratification. Yet, this seemed to blind him to the fact that his students never actually paired together to read. Instead, they formed groups of four to five, and their conversations neglected Cortes, Colombus, and Ponce de Leon and were replaced by video games, reality TV, and that odd new girl who always braided her hair.

As the "reading" continued, Alex questioned his decision to give in. Yes, he was happy for their approval, but began to wonder if it was all just superficial.

—✠—

Day three had started similarly to the first two. Students had begun by "discussing" in small groups the first two questions at the end of the chapter regarding the early European explorers of the Americas. While some groups were on task, most were not. Alex had roamed from group to group striving to keep them focused with friendly reminders like, "Oh, interesting point," and "Let's try to stay focused now." From a distance the scene resembled the old arcade Whack-A-Mole game, for every group Alex whacked back on task, two more popped up.

"Alright guys, back to me please." Alex's mezzo forté call for attention went unnoticed.

"Hey. Right up here please!" His solo swelled to forté, but the audience was still preoccupied with their own performances.

Feeling flustered, Alex planted himself firmly on center stage and bellowed a final fortissimo refrain, "Class! Quiet down!" The audience reluctantly complied.

Empowered

"Thank you. It looks like we've been having some awesome discussions," Alex lied, "and now we're ready to move on. With class almost over, your next goal is to take the remaining questions from this chapter and write a reflection on each for homework. We're looking for at least one typed paragraph for each question due Friday." His off-pitch solo was received with the audience's own mezzo forté chorus of groans and boos – oddly well harmonized too.

One soloist voice rose above while the rest continued in swelling accompaniment. "Come on X-Man, that much by Friday? That's in just two days! How about just the odds?" The chorus grew to a resounding forté with harmonic blends of "yeah," "come on," and "good idea." They sung like a well-rehearsed choir, as if they had previously performed the tune, because, well, they probably had.

The lone man on stage buckled under the pressure. He hung his head and hummed a flat, "Well, alright."

The symphonic band leapt onward in a great climactic celebration. "Awesome!" "Yeah!" "Mr. X is the man!" Though the thunderous reception of his dissonant surrender would have normally thrust him forth with a bow, somehow this time he felt a

> From 2.2.2 – A 'friend' teacher "prioritizes being well-liked over student success."

twinge of guilt. He had previously lived for his audience's applause, yet now it seemed as if their cheering was more for themselves. No, the grand climax wasn't for him; they cheered for the reduction of work.

Yet, it was too late to rewind the performance, so Alex settled for a weakening encore. "With two conditions: They must be full paragraphs and everyone must promise to do it."

Alex was not quite comforted by their off-pitch resolution, "Oh, uh… yeah. We'll try."

—⚘—

"By show of hands, who has begun working on their assignment for chapter one of the textbook?"

Disappointed yet not too terribly surprised to see as many absent hands as bodies in the room, Alex's doubts were confirmed. With only one day left, his mind raced in desperation to find something to motivate his students to fulfill their promise.

> From 2.3.2 – "Extrinsic motivation [is] working to accomplish a goal for the purpose of receiving an external reward."

His mind came back blank, so he let his mouth complete the thought instead. "Alright, how 'bout I give out free tickets to tomorrow's big game if everyone gets it done?"

―⚒―

Friday classes had come and gone, and Alex now sat alone at his desk before heading off to the locker room for his pre-game meetings. He rested his heavy head on a pile of papers, only a few of which were the completed assignments his students had promised him. He kicked himself, near literally, knowing he shouldn't have given out those tickets anyway.

―⚒―

"Long weekend of recovery, coach?" Paul blurted upon noticing Alex enter the teachers' lounge, slumped shoulders and all. "I hear that quarterback ran your D off the field Friday night."

Alex's goal had been to slip in and out unnoticed, after the beating he'd suffered – both on the field and in the classroom. It was Monday's lunchtime, and the first weekend of the school year hadn't done a thing to heal his wounds. That day he had tried to turn around his laissez-faire classroom environment with an entertaining lesson about Columbus's maiden voyage, yet it had fallen flat on his distracted students. Instead, they kept one eye and half their brains focused on the apparently more important matters of note passing, doodling, and checking out that cute someone looking the other way.

Paul's remark, as innocent as it was, felt like another brick heaped on Alex's aching back. He had only intended to quickly snatch his leftover pizza from the fridge and escape to the solitude of his own classroom, but Paul's keen eye and quick mouth forced his temporary interaction by the strong arm of social politeness.

"Yeah, we couldn't keep a read on him. He was quick, man."

"You know, this is yet another reason to stick with bowling, a real man's sport," Paul replied, unaware of Alex's fading self-confidence. "It's all offense."

With a smirk and a nod, Alex relieved himself from further dialogue and stepped toward his escape. Yet before ducking out the door, he peeked back over his shoulder and quickly scanned the room. No one noticed him; no one seemed to care. His eyes then further penetrated the crowd and instinctively found, who he deemed, the leader of the pack. Mrs. Trisha LaValle sat alone, content in her kingdom, sipping pink lemonade with pursed lips and peering intently through thin wire-framed glasses at some scholarly article which was sure to be well over his head. To Alex, she was intelligent, professional, and successful. And like all the rest, Trisha was above him in most every respect, well, the ones that were worth something anyway.

Alex saw himself misplaced, lost in a world of intellectuals. In his own self-depreciating mind, Trisha's persona seeped from her and spread to the entire room, typecasting all as the same. In his judgment, they were all smart, gifted, articulate, and productive. Alex? Mediocre. He labeled himself through his judgment of them. These devaluing sentiments pushed him to seek company in loneliness. He dropped his head in defeat and slipped out the door to the busy hallway beyond.

Alex meandered down the hall with his eyes glued to the tile floor beneath his sneakers. When rounding the corner by the music room, he blindly stepped forward and intersected the path of Kris, the new school counselor. His distracted driving caused a comical crash, yet luckily Kris, quick on her feet, dodged the worst of it. After some cordial apologies, Alex regrouped, looked down, and continued marching in isolation. Though Kris didn't know him, her perceptive eye readily recognized the ball and chain he dragged behind. So, as was her habit, Kris skipped to catch up with her morose associate and walked in step, intent on spreading some sunshine.

"You must be the history teacher, Mr. Clemmington," Kris stated with a friendly tone. "I'm Kris, the new school counselor. Being new here, I've tried to touch base with every teacher; I just haven't made it to the social studies department yet, but I hear good things!"

Alex felt somewhat encouraged by the pleasant reception and Kris's kind disposition. "Well, thank you. And yeah, I'm Alex, football and history here at East Crossroads runnin' five years strong."

As they strolled through the hall, the pleasantries continued in a typical manner one would expect with an initial interaction such as this. They eventually slowed to a stop by the welcoming ceiling-to-floor windows of the Counselor Corner where Kris continued to ask Alex questions, showing interest in that which interested him. It didn't take long for his smile to return, for all he needed was a friendly associate to boost his hidden, volatile emotions.

Yet, just when nearing the point of goodbye, the two were interrupted by the distinct sound of a student conversation just around the corner.

"Second period history? What a joke."

"Mr. X? Please. More like Mr. Y, as in, why is he still here?"

"I know man, he tries to be like us, but that's hard to do when you're twice our age and you've got more hair on your face than your head. What a goober!"

> From 2.1 – "The cords that permit a teacher to lead students are only as strong as their relationship."

Alex's ears burned at the trashing of his name like it belonged in the dumpsters out back. His heart dropped to his feet and his stomach jumped to his throat. Hurt and embarrassed, Alex looked up shyly, wishing the improbable that Kris would be gone. But there she stood, catching Alex's eye with a look of concern and compassion. Self-ostracized from adults, now kicked while down by his students, Alex's pain threatened to surface in a manner unbefitting a championship MVP. So, what could he do in such a situation? He blinked back his grief and released himself from Kris's company with a shrug of his shoulders before disappearing around the corner, never saying a word.

Kris stood still, frozen in place and staring at the empty spot where Alex's empty heart had just been. Within her swelled empathy and concern for this man who seemingly had good intentions but was clearly struggling to fulfill them.

Her thoughts were interrupted by the approaching stomps of Mr. Phippen's size fourteens rounding the same corner where Alex had just vanished. He ambled his way toward her with an inquisitive look, obviously having noticed the history teacher fleeing the scene.

"Hi Kris. Is everything, okay… uh, alright?"

Completely lost in thought, Kris didn't even notice Mr. Phippen's presence. Her eyes remained fixed on an imaginary target while her mind busied itself in analysis and planning. Mr. Phippen pulled back, unwilling to disturb Kris's fierce contemplation yet utterly confused at the meaning of the scene. And as she turned into the Counselor Corner, Kris's passing remark to herself did nothing to dispel his confusion.

"I might need to pick up some more chocolate."

After the hurtful and embarrassing hallway incident, for the rest of the day Alex battled his emotions like a furious fourth quarter goal line stand. The enemy pressed him backward toward doubt and defeat, yet he rallied his inner-forces and battled to remain confident. And as the opponent pushed closer to its target, he admirably maintained an outward appearance of what the inner was trying to achieve.

And, of course, he avoided Kris like she was an All-Pro linebacker.

As the day pressed onward, his inner struggle broke out into a new game – emotional tug-of-war. He came to school the following morning with a confident pull of the rope in his direction, for he had stayed up much of the night running through some much needed positive self-talk.

Yet, upon his walking into class, the rope was pulled back at the sight of the stacks of cluttered papers and empty desks that would soon be filled by unruly teenagers. But today he was determined to conquer his doubt, so he raced around the room and tidied up the mess while reciting his strengths, jerking the rope back in his favor.

As the warning bell drew near and the room approached order, Alex stepped back to his desk to gather his thoughts before the day began. He gazed up at his trophy as a last reminder of his worth, that he could be an MVP of football, teaching, and tug-of-war. When he turned back around in his chair, he noticed something new waiting for him upon a stack of papers in the middle of his desk. It was some bright, foreign object half-wrapped in a small, decorative lavender paper with the ends of the object poking out on the either side. Caught off guard yet clearly curious, Alex reached for it and removed the wrapping to find, to his surprise, a fun sized KitKat bar. This unexpected gift brought a smile to his face. He broke the seal, took a bite, and reached for the purple note.

It read, *"Come chat. ~Kris."*

He dropped the rope.

Alex bombed each class that day as the fear of Kris's motives raced around his weakening mind. How could he go see her? She knew his secret; she knew the truth. She had heard the conversation in the hallway. Surely she fit right in with all the scholars and professionals; did she just want to rub it in?

But wait. What if she was on his side of the rope? What if she could help? She seemed nice; what if she were on his team? And thus he "self-talked" himself all the way to Kris's door after school.

"Well, hello Alex! Come in!"

Kris looked up from some reports on her desk at the sound of Alex's restrained knock on the already opened door. Though her cheerful welcome somewhat calmed him, he still entered timidly.

"I'm thrilled you came by!" Kris related. "I've been hoping to touch base with you."

"And probably more since that awkward incident yesterday after lunch," Alex mumbled.

Kris's friendly countenance became a little more serious to match the mood of her guest. "Well, yes; that too. I've got to tell you, Alex, that such comments go around about most of us. It's just one of those things. And you know, these middle schoolers are still maturing; they're still making that huge transition toward independence and self-discovery. Most of that stuff is just attention seeking behavior. And oh boy, could I tell you some stories from my teaching days!"

Alex sat a little taller in the white leather chair opposite the counselor.

"The unfortunate part is," Kris continued, "that not only are such comments commonplace, but it's also common for even the strongest of teachers to take them a little personally. I mean, how could you not? You wouldn't be a teacher if you didn't care, at least not a very good one anyway."

A shy smile pierced Alex's once solemn countenance. Having Kris tugging on his side of the rope helped them take back the advantage together.

"I suppose it's nice to know I'm not the only one."

Now feeling more comfortable, his reservations relaxed. Whether it was the cushy chairs, bright office, fruity candy, or amiable company, there was something about the situation that set Alex at ease. And as his reservations began to loosen, so did his tongue. He began to feel comfortable enough to reveal his hidden inadequacies, trusting that they would remain safe with this newfound confidant.

"You know, this is my fifth year teaching, and sometimes I still feel like it's my first."

Alex waited for Kris to interject, as would be natural. Yet remaining silent, she urged him onward with a smile. He took the cue, breathed deeply, and continued.

"I got into teaching because I like kids. You know, I wanted to help them enjoy school, enjoy bein' young. Each year I've tried to be cool and make things fun."

"How do you feel that's gone for you?"

Alex rolled his eyes and released a dry chuckle. "You'd like to think that these kids, whose lives revolve around fun, would enjoy a teacher who likes to have fun! I used to think we were gettin' somewhere, but now I see that we're stuck. I'm a runnin' back tryin' to move the D-line by myself, man. We're gettin' nowhere, especially my second period."

"Boy, five years of this. That's got to be tough, especially since you really care."

"Yeah! I know!" yelped Alex. "It's like the nicer I am the less serious they take me. I don't get it. I joke. I laugh. I even give out free tickets to the games!"

The more Alex talked, the more animated he became. His gaze soon zeroed in on the bare wall to the side, becoming less aware of his immediate environment and more lost in the built up emotions he'd been battling. The wear and tear on his ego flowed outward like a waterslide; now that it had begun, there was no slowing down.

"It seems like no matter what I do, I just can't get them on my side. Five years of this!" Alex's vision bore holes in the blank wall as he continued to zip down the slippery slide. "It's just like in high school; no different at all. Even with them, the harder I tried to fit in on the team, the farther down the bench they'd push me! Every effort got thrown back in my face."

Then the splash in the pool below. "I'm the backup punter all over again!"

Kris's valiant effort to keep up had been successful enough, until this last disclosure. "Excuse me, backup punter?"

Alex recoiled. His eyes flashed forward to Kris then instinctively shot down to the floor, realizing his inadvertent confession. He rocked slightly in his chair and rubbed his arms, as if toweling off.

"Well, uh, yeah." He slowly continued. "As embarrassing as it is, it's even more embarrassing to admit out loud. So, yeah, if you read those framed newspaper articles in my classroom, my name's not there. And that trophy? Garage sale. The truth is that I was never 'Superstar X.' You're looking at 'Alexander Clemmington,' the backup punter of the high school football team. Benchwarmer. Loser. I barely even played because our team scored on pretty much every possession."

Kris couldn't help but feel the need to stifle an oncoming smile at this unexpected twist. Yet still, she kept her composure with her natural compassion for Alex's struggle.

"So to compensate, you've now gone to the other extreme."

"Yeah, come to think of it, I guess I've become what I hated as a teenager."

"Popularity and fun over determination and success."

The two sat back for a moment to soak it all in. Kris looked down at her ceramic candy dish on the table between them, taking note of the pile of wrappers off to the side. Clearly, the fruity stuff wasn't doing the job. So, she reached into the side drawer and pulled out a couple of KitKats. Alex accepted the offering, and the two crunched together in time, content in their own thoughts for the moment.

> From 2.2.1 – "The teacher must be the consummate and consistent example."

Once both bars were consumed, Alex looked down at his hands and flexed them a few times, as if preparing to grab hold of a rope.

"Wow, what an eye opener. I guess I've never really taken the time to think this all through. I'm goin' about it all wrong, aren't I?"

"Alex," Kris replied at this opportune moment, "it's pretty clear to me that your desires have been sincere, but you're right, perhaps your methods have been misguided. Let me tell you, students generally perform to the measure of their immediate environment, whether high or low. It appears to me that the expectations in your class, both for behavior and academics, haven't been as high as they could be."

The coach nodded in agreement.

"Now, when you set your expectations high, the students are more likely to live up to them if you've created a strong, professional bond. The cords that permit a teacher to lead students are only as strong as their relationship of respect and trust. The stronger the relationship, the more they'll follow."

Alex listened intently, understanding the words but struggling to visualize them in action. "Okay, but haven't I been trying to do that? I try each day to make them like me, and it hasn't gotten me anywhere."

"You're right; it hasn't. So, think about what you just said. 'I try to make them like me.' I never told you to make them like you."

"You told me," Alex interjected, his eyes lighting up with understanding, "to build a relationship of respect and trust. The two are quite different, aren't they?"

Kris smiled at his progress. "Exactly. Merely liking your teacher is similar to liking a friend. Do you think it's worthwhile for them to treat you similar to a peer?"

"No."

"Neither do I. Your relationship should be based on respect and trust, not partying and football. They should view you as a friendly, approachable professional. They should understand that you care for their future as much as you care for their present. You honor them by honoring your position."

"Sounds boring. When I was in school, my favorite teachers were the cool ones."

"Yes, you may have *liked* them the most, but did you *succeed* the most in those classes?"

Alex didn't respond as he tried to grasp the impact of the question. Yet, Kris continued without a response, understanding that he knew the inevitable answer. "Again Alex, there's a difference. Now, I want you to do something for me. We've made great progress in our little discussion today, but now we need to take it one step further."

Alex's eyes narrowed into focus.

"A trick I've found to be most useful over the years is to journal. Writing down my thoughts seems to have a way of providing clarity and direction. May I suggest you give that a try? If I were in your shoes, I would jot down the difference between the terms 'friendly' and 'friends' and how particular aspects of my teaching style fit into each."

"A writing assignment, huh?" Alex responded. "I've been out of college for a while; I might be a bit rusty. But okay, I think I can give it shot."

"I tell you what. I'll simplify this first entry by providing a few guiding questions."

The two wrapped up their conversation with some particulars of the assignment. Upon leaving, Alex felt quite different than when he had entered. He now stepped strong, feeling validated, understood, and resolved with a new sense of direction.

Journal Entry – September 2

Why is a strong teacher/student relationship important? *My five years of experience show the negative effects of a weak relationship. My students haven't trusted me enough to listen or follow. Honestly, we've just been puttering along, learning a little but mostly just killing time until the next break. If I can change my ways enough to build stronger relationships, then they should be more motivated. Then maybe they'll listen, respond, and achieve a little more.*

> From 2.1 –
> "Relationships of respect and trust provide the necessary motivation for a student to raise their personal expectations."

How does a "friend" teacher act? *This describes my first five years. Trying to be funny and modern, I interacted more as a peer than a mentor. I never really held students accountable. I desired being liked more than their academic success. For some reason, I thought if I were cool, they'd like me enough to listen. Instead, they just lived up to my low expectations.*

How does a "friendly" teacher act? *This is what I need to become. A friendly teacher interacts as a willing mentor and is warm, happy, and approachable* while still holding students accountable. Our friendly relationships should encourage and focus on their success.

How can I be both "friendly" and "professional"? To set the example, I've got to be even better than what I expect of my students. I need to take my job more seriously. I need to be more timely in my grading, thorough in my feedback, and available for discussion. I need to better organize my classroom and use my instructional time. And yet, I should do all this while being cheerful and approachable, not morphing into some sort of unrelatable, robotic stiff. This should demonstrate to students my commitment to both my position and their success.

How will this improve my classroom culture? Students will come to class with a better understanding of our purpose and a desire to really go for it. With this professional yet friendly approach to my position, I hope that they'll come to class to learn instead of play. We can still enjoy ourselves, but for the right purpose.

"Please, tell me I don't have to wear a tie!"

Kris looked up from her computer to see Alex, a little flustered, bursting into her office.

"Good afternoon, Alex," Kris replied, happy to see the coach. "I can see you've been doing some reflecting. How's the journal coming?"

"Terrible! I've been writing and thinking about this for days. I can't tell you how much I've learned!"

Kris scratched her puzzled brow. "What's so terrible about that?"

"Because I've come to a conclusion, a terribly difficult conclusion." Alex found his way to one of the white, leather chairs and gathered himself with a deep breath. "Kris, all this means that I have to change, doesn't it?"

Kris's first reply was to stand up from behind her desk and maneuver over to the single chair. She looked across the room, proud of what she saw. It was clear from Alex's demeanor that he had taken the journaling assignment seriously, and it had obviously had an effect.

"Well, I never told you to wear a tie. Do *you* think you need to wear a tie?"

"Since my first journal entry, and all the thinking between then and now, I've realized I haven't been an adult. I haven't taken my job or the students seriously. I haven't even taken myself seriously. This is the real game, and I've been sitting on the bench."

As Alex continued to summarize the main points of his honest self-reflection, Kris marveled at his insights. It was clear he understood, at least conceptually, what it meant to be friendly and professional. He understood the necessity of relationships of respect and trust.

"Kris, I believe I'm beginning to see what my students need me to be. And that's what's so scary. Since I'm not currently that teacher they need, it means I have to change."

"And change is hard."

"Change is terrible. Ties are terrible!"

"So, what's wrong with wearing a tie?"

Alex lowered his voice for emphasis. "It's not so much the tie as it is what the tie represents." He breathed deep and concluded in a whisper, "If I want my students to take their education seriously, I need to take it seriously too."

Kris's elation shined bright through her eager smile. "Well coach, just look at you! You're beginning to sound like a teacher!"

Alex's sheepish expression in return confirmed his pleasure from the compliment.

Kris continued, "Alex, you'll still be fun and cool, but you'll also be encouraging. You'll be motivating. You'll be happy, approachable, and professional. You'll be someone your students want to emulate. Tie or no tie, you will create a classroom environment focused on student success."

Alex stood and moved toward the door. "A new culture. I can see it; I can even see how to do it. It's just the actual doing of it that scares me.

I've been teaching this way for so long, how can I just snap my fingers and change?"

Kris also stood and joined Alex at the exit. "Well, how do you score a touchdown?"

Alex smiled at his mentor's simplicity. "One yard at a time."

Change. Why is change so hard? Green leaves change to red. Winter changes to spring. Night changes to day. But a man can't put his wallet in the other back pocket. He can't wear his watch on the other wrist. He can't bring himself to drive a different route to work. Yes, he can identify a bad habit, but he has the hardest time changing what he knows he should. While the world seems able to cope with change, he who inhabits the world separates himself by – not.

Alex sat at his desk the following Monday morning, suppressing his anxiety and feeling uncomfortable with the changes he surveyed before him. The evidence of his work the previous weekend was apparent all around. Clean desk. Organized bookshelves. Clear directions written on the board. Copies of assignments for the next two weeks neatly filed away.

> From 2.2.1 – "A professional approach will demonstrate to students your commitment to your position and thus your respect for their time and confidence in their efforts."

Scanning the walls, the absence of the previously present sports memorabilia reminded Alex of some other missing decorations, the most important decorations. There was no need to turn around and look up, for Alex could feel the empty shelf above him calling out the absence of his fake shrine. No newspapers. No self-portraits. No garage sale trophies. As challenging as it was, Alex had done it; he had taken down his false memories. They represented his past, and now he had committed himself to change.

As the time approached for his students to enter, Alex stood to ready the last details of the day. The movement forced a swish of color to pass through his periphery. He looked down and frowned to see his old, skinny maroon tie he hadn't seen since senior prom and wished he would have never seen again. Yet there it was, flopping about, exaggerating each movement and mocking him at every turn. To him, the tie was like a pesky little sister, irritating and inescapable.

And though he'd been able to remember how to tie it, he still refused to tighten it all the way up. Hey, a man's got to draw the line somewhere!

> From 2.2.1 – "Dress and groom yourself in a manner that reflects the spirit of your classroom expectations."

With the ring of the warning bell, students began to enter. First, the front row dwellers quietly slipped in. They barely got inside before noticing the room's transformation. Their eyes grew large at seeing the drastic changes. They quickly took their seats, but not without giving each other some quizzical looks.

The middle tier had a similar reaction. Yet the football crew, fresh off their recent victory, made their boisterous entrance like a pack of yipping dogs. Absorbed in reliving their teenage glory, they made their way to the back as usual without noticing a thing.

"Good morning, class!" Alex called for attention in a pleasant tone, trying to hold his tie in place. "You're all looking like you've had a good weekend and are ready to learn. As you can see on the board, today we'll be…"

"Yo coach!" interrupted a burly boy from the football table. "What's with the ratty tie?"

Alex had anticipated the comment, so he was prepared with a witty response. "Yes, you like it, don't you?" He picked it up and stroked its smooth surface as if petting a dog. "I'm glad you noticed this archaic beauty and all its vintage qualities. This is history class after all, and this thing is a living artifact!"

The class let out an honest chuckle, relieved to see that the sudden change in their teacher's appearance hadn't totally changed his character. Alex let the tie fall back into place and smiled as the laughter died down.

"Now, as you look around, you'll notice some changes, including, of course, my new choker. The last several days I've been researching and reflecting on our first few weeks of school, and honestly, I can't help but feel that we haven't accomplished as much as we should have by now. But at this point, I primarily blame myself. So class," Alex reached out one arm gesturing to the room transformation while the other held back up his tie, "it's time for a little change, and I thought I'd start with myself."

> From 2.2.2 – "It is possible to be professional and friendly, but it is not possible to be professional and friends."

Alex paused, expecting some sort of reaction, but the class remained silent. They still seemed to be processing this new information, which was taking longer than expected since thinking wasn't something they were accustomed to doing in history class.

Alex gulped hard and continued with forced confidence. "I'm excited for the rest of this year. While cleaning over the weekend, I came up with some great ideas, especially for our next unit on the early American colonies. Now, we won't get started until next week, but here's a hint… we're going to be establishing our own class colonies patterned after the original thirteen. Settling, farming, fishing, religion, leadership, and of course… money!"

A small stir of anticipation rippled throughout the class. Their reaction told Alex he had piqued their interest, but it was still clear that their excitement was somewhat restrained, probably due to Alex's long-standing "read-the-text-answer-the-questions" style. To them, the idea was intriguing, but was it for real?

"I'm still planning out the details, but I'm pretty confident you'll enjoy it. We'll learn lots and make it meaningful by applying it all to your own lives. It's going to take some work, but we've got a great group of students here who, I'm sure, are up to the challenge. And if I can wear this purple beast for a change, you guys can do great with this activity."

The students looked around at their classmates, not really knowing what to think. They liked the thought of getting out from behind the textbook, but the prospect of more work didn't sound too pleasant. They silently weighed the cons of challenge and effort versus the pros of something new and engaging.

> <u>From 4.2.3</u> – A student-centered teacher employs "engaging lessons for the purpose of learning concepts."

Alex left his classroom after fourth period feeling pretty good about himself; his tie wasn't quite the noose it was that morning. The day hadn't been perfect, especially his second period, but overall things went well. Students had listened, participated, and seemed genuinely interested in the upcoming colony unit. Frankly, it had all gone better than expected.

Heading passed the Counselor Corner toward the teachers' lounge to grab his lunch, Alex felt a sudden surge of trepidation. He had just left the cozy confines of his classroom where he had exhibited newfound control. There, his future felt bright. There, he was creating a stronger identity. The lounge, however, engendered many feelings where, ironically enough, none of which were comfortable. Anxiety, apprehension, angst… Alex's self-judgment through the eyes of his peers seemed to increase his new attire's choke hold around his neck.

Alex breathed in deeply, summoning the confidence necessary to conquer his fear. They were just larger versions of his students; what was the big deal? So Alex resolved to boldly step forth to the battle field, his maroon banner waving unabashed to his foe – and secretly step to the fridge, snatch his lunch, and dash out unnoticed.

Hey, baby steps, right?

Acting on his plan of stealth, Alex slipped through the cracked door and headed for the fridge. Yet while in route, Paul, of course, was the first to spy the sneaky shadow.

"Well, check you out, Mr. GQ himself. Looking sharp today! What's with the new look, coach?"

Alex, pinned against the wall half-way to his escape, sheepishly replied, "Oh, no big deal. Just trying something new."

"You too? That new language arts teacher has been going on – and on – about all the changes in her room as well. But it looks like she beat you to it; this is just her first year!"

Alex inched his way closer to freedom. "Is that right? Well yeah, that's uh, good for her."

"Did that new counselor get to you too?" Paul mercilessly persisted. "She sure seems to have a way of bowling on someone else's lane."

Alex finally made it to the exit and left with a muted, mumbled response. "Well, if she helps you get a strike."

Journal Entry – September 16

We're a week into the colony unit and two weeks since I've started to clean myself up. Those first few days turned out to be much more difficult than I thought. After that first day went so well, I thought I was set, but that was certainly not the case. Since then they have really tried to push my buttons. Perhaps I'm exaggerating, but it seems like they fought me at every opportunity. Especially second period, with each request, I received battle in return.

Take Wednesday for instance. After a good class discussion on the early relations between the European settlers and Native Americans, I asked half the class to write a reflection from the perspective of the settlers and the other half from the perspective of the natives. Oh, how they whined! Fourth period was alright, but second period nearly revolted!

By Thursday I was ready to give up. I'd been trying to be friendly and professional, but it just wasn't working. And the worst thing about it was that the more they fought me, the more I grew to hate my tie. That stupid piece of fabric seemed to embody all my frustrations. Talking – stupid tie. Whining – idiotic tie. Half effort – insanely ridiculous scrap of silk! (Side note – why silk anyway? I'm a football player. Tough guys don't wear silk!)

And speaking of whining, I did so to Kris. Luckily she's more patient than I. She told me that it was natural for students to push back and test their boundaries. They had several weeks with the old, kick-back Mr. X. They were settled. Now all of the sudden Mr. Clemmington shows up disturbing the peace.

She gave me two pieces of really good advice. First, as much as I hated it at the time, she told me to stay the course. Don't give in. Don't let the boundaries and budding professional relationships crumble just as you're getting started. She compared it to popping popcorn. You've got to create firm boundaries and expectations so the kernels can pop inside. Building relationships of respect and trust reinforce the boundaries. (Another side note - Come to think of it, is that what Sheri was rambling about last week?)

The second was so easy, I'm surprised I didn't think of it earlier. She told me to make regular positive contacts with individual students. She taught me the "Quadruple P" model of interacting with students to strengthen relations: purposeful, personalized, positive, and professional. She said how routinely seeking out opportunities to treat students as exceptional individuals within the normal context of school would strengthen the cords of respect and trust, and thus the classroom culture.

> From 2.2.3 – "If a student is treated as just one of the masses, the relationship (or lack thereof) will reflect it."

So, I set out to do some "QP" interactions each day, targeting the ring leaders first, as Kris suggested. Some students I verbally complimented about some-

thing unique to them while to others I wrote a little note. Some I even called or emailed their parents for the sole purpose of telling them something good about their kid. One mom was so used to getting calls about her son's misbehavior that she about had a heart attack when I called with only a compliment!

So, how's it going now? I'd love to say they're great. I'd love to say everything is Super Bowl Sunday perfect. Yet while I certainly can't go that far, I am pleased to report that things are, well, better. The students seem to fight me less. The whining has reduced a fair amount. I can't get everyone to participate fully, but it's safe to say a lot more are with me.

What's really interesting is that the ring leaders seem to now be helping more than hurting. Take Laurie in third period for example. She used to ignore the lesson and pay attention to everything and everyone else. Now, just yesterday, I caught her shushing her table so she could better hear a group presentation. Way cool.

And our colony unit has been a blast. Honestly, it's pretty hard leaving the textbook; that's been my whole curriculum for so long (or maybe my crutch for so long). Though leaving that safety zone and coming up with new ideas has been tough, the students are really responding well. Most seem more eager to participate.

That is, everyone except second period.

While all my other classes are moving upward, these kids refuse to budge. They're so stubborn and completely resistant to change. (Come to think of it, they are quite a bit like me!) As an example, earlier this week we spent the day researching the primary religious convictions in the colonies and how it affected their culture and politics. You'd think I had hired a firing squad to pick them off one by one! No motivation and no action, just whining and off task chatting.

I was at a loss, so I resorted to bribery again. I told them if they stepped it up, their unit test would be open book, but that's not what they wanted. Instead they campaigned for some sort of "Fun Friday," complete with games, food, and free time. Kris will probably kill me, but at the time I figured, why not? A free day in exchange for a week of quality work? Seems worthwhile enough.

Overall, I'm feeling pretty good. I just wish change came a little more quickly. (Now, off to practice – where I finally get to ditch this tie!)

"But it worked! They worked! As idiotic as our Fun Friday was, for some reason it motivated my second period to actually take the colony project somewhat seriously. Whatever happened to a little give and take?"

One morning, Kris had stopped by Alex's classroom a few days after the completion of the colony unit. She wanted to check in on his progress and offer her compliments and encouragement; however, it hadn't turned out the way she anticipated. Their conversation progressed like the dramatic sequence of an adventure novel. The plot was introduced with Alex reporting his students' small progress combined with moments of vivid conflict. The story thickened with the complaining and defiance of second period, tension mounting with the turn of each page. And as the bludgeoning challenge rolled forth, his epic conquest climaxed as he surmounted the gargantuan feat by taming his unruly second period creature at great peril and self-sacrifice, all with the unlikely yet cunning stratagem that was, "Fun Friday." Yes, the duty was done, and to the victor goes the crown.

Or so he thought.

Without meaning to fully dethrone this conquistador, Kris revealed a surprise ending to Alex's seemingly triumphant tale – bribing the dragon only satisfies the beast temporarily. Hence, Alex's defensive reaction; he simply wasn't prepared for a sequel.

So Kris proceeded carefully, knowing that she was treading on sensitive ground. "Alex, are you familiar with the old adage about giving a man a fish versus teaching him to fish?"

"Yeah," Alex grunted, still sulking.

Kris noted his tone but hoped to soon see a crack in Alex's stony façade. "The one option feeds the man for a day while the other feeds him for a life. Would you agree the latter is the better option?"

Alex replied with a slight nod.

"Now, your Fun Friday is what we'd call extrinsic motivation. You couldn't get your class to go fishing, so you tossed them their dinner. They liked it. You liked it. It tasted good. Everyone was well fed and felt good about themselves. But what will happen tomorrow?"

Alex stirred in his chair and begrudgingly admitted the obvious answer. "They'll be hungry again."

"Exactly!" exclaimed Kris, happy to see Alex's awareness. "And what will happen if you keep tossing them fish each day?"

> From 2.3.2 – Extrinsic motivation "may produce desired results in the short term, but it does not build long term, sustainable self-motivation."

"Well," Alex answered, now beginning to grasp the idea, "I guess they'll stay fed as long as they're with me, but they'll go hungry once they move on."

Kris sat back in her chair and gazed across the table with an approving grin. "Look at you! You're much sharper than you give yourself credit."

Pleased by the compliment, Alex sat tall and replied, "It must have been all that time on the bench instead of in the game. Less hits to the head!"

The two enjoyed a hearty laugh at Alex's joke, which prompted Kris to conclude that the setting had become ripe to proceed. "Now Alex, we've talked much the last several weeks about building relationships of respect and trust with your students, the purpose of which is to strengthen your classroom culture of success. You've done wonderfully thus far building relationships through friendly professionalism and QP contacts, but now you have another lesson to learn."

Alex's focused stare was all Kris needed to continue.

"The strength of your relationship will only be as strong as your students' motivation to follow you. If their motivation is weak, it doesn't matter where you're leading. If it's strong, they'll follow you anywhere. Thus, employing proper methods of motivation will greatly strengthen your relationship and subsequently your classroom culture of success."

"And just dangling a fish in front of them is only motivating for so long," Alex interjected.

"Right on! That method is called 'extrinsic motivation.' This is where students work to accomplish a goal for the purpose of receiving an external reward, like a pizza party, free time, or avoiding a punishment. Though this may give you immediate results, it doesn't last.

"Now teaching them to fish is called 'intrinsic motivation.' This is where students work to accomplish a goal for the purpose of receiving an internal reward, like knowledge, personal satisfaction, or a sense of accomplishment. This may or may not produce immediate results, but it most certainly will create that long term, sustainable self-motivation we want."

Alex sat back to digest the concept and another piece of candy.

"Motivating intrinsically," continued Kris, "is where you strive to engender within your students the desire to achieve because they want to achieve, because that achievement is in and of itself the best reward. As Fun Fridays aren't always readily available throughout students' lives to push them forward, it is our job, as teachers, to teach them to push themselves."

Alex looked around his newly organized classroom. These last few weeks had been harder than any of his career. Aside from the effort it took to clean up his mess, the time and mental energy he'd exerted rivaled that of any dragon-slaying hero. This culture business was hard work.

"It's just so much easier to give them a fish," Alex confessed. "You don't have to show him how to bait the hook, cast the line, wait patiently, and reel it in. Sometimes it's easier to just do it yourself and hand the man his dinner."

"Now believe me Alex," Kris interjected, "I understand the challenge; I did it for fifteen years. But it shouldn't be a question of difficulty, instead it's a question of effectiveness. What is best for my students? What can I do that will be of most value to them? Is it bribing them so they put forth the minimal amount of effort on a colony unit in order to gain a prize? Or is it building within them an inner desire to achieve, a feeling of self-confidence, a sense of motivation that will propel them to long-term success, even at the possible expense of a mediocre colony unit now?"

Alex flipped through a stack of crinkled colony presentations and gazed right through their superficial and inflated design. His students had produced these; they had accomplished what he asked of them, but he now understood that they ought to have accomplished something greater that they asked of themselves.

Shoving the stack back in the black plastic tray labeled "Second Period," Alex's mind raced through this surprise turn of events at the conclusion of his adventure story. The action had peaked and dove in a new direction, and now he foresaw the grand conclusion just around the corner. Yes, his students did learn and achieve, but they learned and achieved a smaller lesson. Accelerating to the conclusion, Alex envisioned something larger in store for his students, something better. The novel arrived at its surprising secondary climax – he'd teach his students... *to fish*!

Alex blinked his eyes back into focus and shyly looked around. A sense of relief swelled within at the realization that this time he was able to contain within his mind this last emotional outburst – unlike his backup punter confession a few weeks ago.

Reeling in his emotions, Alex cast out the obvious next question, "So, how exactly do I build intrinsic motivation?"

"The first step is to stop using extrinsic motivators."

"Stop completely?"

"If you're trying to build on the *inside* of students, use *intrinsic* motivators. This ought to be the standard approach. There may be times in abnormal circumstances where an extrinsic motivator may be appropriate, but be sure to wean it away as soon as possible."

"Like when?"

"Consider the example of a student who rarely completes his homework and isn't influenced by poor grades or other consequences. You could cut him some sort of deal to gain a particular prize of value to him if he meets a certain goal. Once he's succeeded and you've had the opportunity to praise him for his efforts, and he's had opportunity to experience the rewards of completing his work, gradually wean him away from the prize. Use the extrinsic to give the intrinsic a chance, then take the extrinsic away so he doesn't become dependent. After all, the starving man might not even know he likes fish until you give him a taste."

"Okay, got it. Intrinsic is the default. Extrinsic is the exception. What else?"

"I wish I could give you a simple trick, but it's not that easy. The good news is, however, that you're well on your way already. Building intrinsic motivation necessitates creating a culture of success. Such a culture comes with high expectations, good relationships, reinforcing the positive, and student-centered instruction."

As the clock ticked onward, Alex kept casting questions, hungry for more ideas. Yet, they were eventually rudely interrupted by the warning bell.

"I tell you what," Kris said wrapping things up, "I want you to explore the idea of intrinsic motivation some more on your own. Let's see if you can brainstorm a few good strategies, then we can discuss them together."

Alex playfully rolled his eyes like one of his teenage students. "Journal entry?"

"Hasn't that been working for you?" Kris quipped.

Upon saying their goodbyes, Kris ducked out the door just as Alex's budding fishermen angled in and took their seats. He synched up his tie a little more.

Second period's old baggy jeans football coach had made quite the transformation the past few weeks; however, the unfortunate combination of students created a class dynamic resistant to the change. Oh sure, the students had made some progress, but it seemed a drop in the bucket compared to where they could be. They were simply an unmotivated group.

And five minutes into class that day, they continued to resist their teacher's dynamic presentation on the rising resistance leading up to the Revolutionary War. Despite the interesting topic and their teacher's engaging lesson, their attention found their friends instead.

"Alright, today we're in for a little treat," announced Alex stroking his tie, now a habit. "We're going to watch a small video clip chronicling some of the key instigators of the uprising." Several students shouted with excitement at the thought of a video in class, which caught the attention of the rest who hadn't been listening.

The students hushed at the dimming of the lights. After hitting play, Alex roamed among the students as they watched the video. He was pleased at their attentiveness. It wasn't that the video itself was exceptionally engaging, but it was the change of pace that brought them all together.

Five minutes in, Alex hit stop and flicked on the lights. The sudden change back to normal caught the students off guard. They howled in protest.

> From 2.2.1 – "Maximize instructional time."

"Come on Mr. Clemmington! That was a cool video! Can't we watch the rest?"

Alex caught himself before letting words escape his lips, knowing that he couldn't take them back once released. He had never intended to show more than five minutes because he wanted to reserve the time for another activity he had specifically planned for this group, having thought through some details of intrinsic motivation. Perhaps he should have warned them he'd stop the video early, but it was too late now.

Unlike the second day of school where they pleaded to read from the textbook with a partner, he determined to not give in. But he was, however, tempted to offer more video time at the end of class for good behavior. The extrinsic bribe seemed rather harmless, but he concluded he needed to follow through on his plans to test the intrinsic fishing waters.

"Yeah, that was interesting, wasn't it?" Alex conveyed with a hearty grin, "and we have another activity in store that should bring this conflict to life." He ignored the peppering of persistent moans and continued. "We've learned for a few days how this revolutionary tension began to build. And now it's time to put ourselves directly in the rebellion, right in the midst of the video ourselves."

> From 3.3 – "Most student behaviors, even misbehaviors, can simply be ignored."

Alex's perceptive glance noticed that now most eyes stared back attentively. Some even leaned forward on their seats with anticipation.

"You guys, my second period students," he paused for effect, "are going to instigate – a fight. You're going to be the recruiters to rally troops to your cause. There's a war to be had, and you're going to lead us!"

A wave of energy rippled across the class. Their reactions, curious and excited, communicated their desire for more. So, Alex uncovered a short series of directions prewritten on the board.

"Your objective is to prepare a short rallying cry to persuade fellow settlers to join your cause of revolution. You'll have ten minutes to plan. How long?"

"Ten minutes!"

"Your speech much be short, no more than eight sentences. How many sentences?"

"Eight!"

"You'll work with the person sitting directly across from you in your groups – please point to your partner."

All hands found their partner.

"And you must include two to three facts we've reviewed in class that contributed to the revolution. How many facts?"

"Two to three!"

"Now your mission," Alex lowered his tone to build up to the climax of his own rallying cry, "is to recruit as many troops as possible. Use facts that will strike at our hearts: our families, our farms, our liberty. Be concise, be persuasive, and go win us our freedom!"

> From 2.3.3 – "Present material in a manner that engages students' interest. Teach with enthusiasm."

The class burst into action. The sheer excitement of their task propelled them onward to battle, their minds and pencils acting as weapons. Alex roamed throughout the classroom, checking in on each group and offering compliments and suggestions. The video was now erased from their minds as they moved forward with their activity in haste. Alex occasionally called out the remaining time, each reminder causing a new rush of action.

There was only time for half the groups to deliver their speeches that day. Some were better than others, but most had given it their best. At the ring of the dismissal bell, Alex smiled at the complaining groans because it was clear that these groans rung different, for this time they were clearly a compliment for a change.

> From 2.3.1 – "A classroom culture of success is predicated upon students' motivation to follow their teacher."

Journal Entry – October 3

I'm tired. I'm happy, but tired. This classroom culture stuff is both rewarding and challenging. I suppose I wouldn't have had to work as hard if I had started the year off this way, but it's okay, the progress we've made has been worth it. Between organizing my room, preparing and grading more thoroughly, QP contacts, and all this intrinsic motivation, some days I go home with my head spinning as hard as that hit I took my junior year of football. But then again, that punt did pin them inside the five!

Kris was right that there isn't any sort of easy trick to motivate your kids. Take second period as an example. It's been a couple of weeks since that awesome rally cry activity where they were so engaged, and since then we've had just as many bad days as good. But I've kept at it. And as hard as it was, I kept trying to create interesting opportunities for them to be engaged and seek after their own learning. Some worked great, others didn't. But as time keeps passing, I'm beginning to notice how for every three yard sack, we seem to move forward five more on the next play. Progress, I guess, is all I need to keep myself motivated to motivate my students.

Now, through experience and discussion with Kris, I have learned a few strategies to build intrinsic motivation. She, of course, suggested I jot them down. So, here we go.

Set Appropriate and Meaningful Expectations: *Students should be expected to perform to a level that makes them stretch but is not out of reach. Take that rally cry activity, for instance. My first idea was to take two days to compose a full page speech, but these guys needed something a little smaller and quicker. My fourth period, though, handled the longer assignment just fine.*

> From 2.3.3 – "If expectations are too high, they are unreachable, and if too low, accomplishing them is not true success."

Dynamic Presentation: *Those are Kris's words; this football coach could never be so articulate! This means to present material in an engaging manner, getting them hooked through intriguing and innovative methods. For example, contrast my old habit of daily textbook reading to that exciting colony unit (Ah! What had I been thinking?). Also, it's beneficial to show students quality example work that they would want to emulate. Seeing something good they can shoot for has already worked wonders for my kids, second period in particular.*

Self-Monitoring: This is challenging in middle school. These young teens are usually either too hard on themselves or too full of themselves, with not much in between. We need to teach them to be their own best critics, but not to the point of self-depreciation (of which I know something about!). We can provide rubrics, checklists, and sometimes just a little bit of time to self-analyze. I've also noticed that being a model of self-monitoring shows students how to do it and teaches them it's healthy to do so.

Positive Encouragement and Recognition: When they do something well, tell them. I'm beginning to believe Kris's saying that the genuine praise of a trusted adult is worth more than any trinket money can buy. We should also look for ways to celebrate success together as a class, like providing opportunities for students to complement each other. Kris also taught me the value of demonstrating the connection between work and success. This past week I've often found myself telling students, "You can do hard things."

Sharing Accomplishments: When kids have worked hard and been successful, it's important to let them share. The method of doing so depends on the activity. Sometimes they can verbally present to the class, while at other times I might just post their work on the wall. I've thought of a variety of ways to do this, but in the end it doesn't really matter, just as long as I do it. Kris says the time it takes to share student accomplishments multiplies tenfold in building intrinsic value.

Next week we're starting the unit on the creation of our government. I've been brainstorming with teachers in our department some new ideas to teach the Declaration of Independence and the Constitution. I don't have it all nailed down yet, but I'm hoping to spend some time in the school library for individual student research. Oh boy, are they ready for something like that? Am I?

Ah! Let's do it! Let's see how far I can stretch them.

Empowered

Winter was approaching. With the passing months both Alex and his students were now quite comfortable with that ugly silk maroon tie – and all it represented. Alex stood at the front of the room, silently surveying his second period students as they quietly prepared notecards for their upcoming speeches to a fictitious continental congress. Taking a moment to reflect, Alex felt enveloped with a sense of pride, fatherly pride almost, at how far this group had come.

They had sure put up a good fight, much more so than his other classes, but eventually they too had come around. As he approached their education professionally, they had done the same. As he had changed, they changed with him, just as fall was now changing to winter. They were still friendly and enjoyed the occasional joke, but it was different now than at the beginning of the year. Now they could do those things parallel with the lesson, like eating dessert simultaneously with dinner. Relationships of trust had been painstakingly built, and now they reaped the benefits together. They could now mingle learning with a little pleasure, for learning in and of itself had become a pleasure.

"Excuse me, Mr. Clemmington," a boy in a football jersey sitting up front raised his hand. "Class is almost over; isn't it time for daily wrap up?"

Alex awoke from his reverie and glanced at the clock. "Yes, you're right. Thanks Chad. Alright everyone, put your notecards away and take out your day planners. As always, your assignment is on the board. Go ahead and jot it down while I put up the quote of the day."

> From 2.2.2 – A friendly teacher "interacts as a willing mentor [with] high expectations [while holding] students accountable."

Students busily grabbed their planners as Alex projected on the screen a short quote in large, bold lettering. Displayed near the top in small print read, "*Contemplation Quote #13.*"

"When it comes to this class," Alex related, "today's quote has extra special meaning to me. You've come so far this semester, and I see nothing but blue skies ahead. You've demonstrated for weeks your intelligence, dedication, and perseverance. You've been a wonderful example to me. Now, as you contemplate this quote throughout the day, I want you to identify how this is true for you individually. Perhaps a couple of you will even be brave enough to share your thoughts with the class tomorrow. Krista, will you read it for us?"

> From 2.2.2 - A friendly teacher "builds relationships with students that lead to the ultimate goal of their success. [They] encourage and celebrate student success."

Alex stood back and surveyed the students as they all concentrated intently on what had become the closing routine of history class. With only a few exceptions, the pondering and interpreting of powerful quotes from prominent figures in history had produced meaningful insights and motivating applications. Though only taking two or three minutes per day, the contemplation quotes had quickly become a class favorite.

Krista cleared her throat, proud to be acting as voice. "Genius is one percent inspiration and ninety-nine percent perspiration. Accordingly, a 'genius' is often merely a talented person who has done all of his homework. Thomas Edison."

―⁂―

"You're averaging 220 now? Man! We could have used some of your bowling consistency in our football playoffs. Before long you'll be above 250!"

Alex's friendly compliment brought a smile to Paul's wrinkled face.

"Yeah, I've even cut back a bit on league play," replied Paul, sipping hot chocolate. "Something must be in the air, or maybe it's my new daily dose of chocolate milk!"

The teachers' lounge had become a little more crowded these days since Mr. Phippen had produced this year's Christmas bonus a couple weeks early – a hot chocolate maker. As the days cooled down, this once scoffed at budget-strapped "bonus" became a little more endearing. But

Alex continued to slurp his daily sports drink, content to be surrounded by good company.

Alex now dined daily in the lounge with his colleagues. What once seemed like a traumatic feat was now customary, natural even. He'd realized that as his classroom culture strengthened, so did his self-confidence. His hidden emotional ups and downs had ebbed and flowed right out the door. Success, he garnered, strengthens confidence, a newfound trait that finally allowed him self-admittance to the high society of his colleague professionals.

But now that he had joined the club, he became more aware of the futility of his once self-demeaning ways. They were just like him. Trying, yet not fully arrived. Dedicated, yet occasionally fallible. Successful, yet imperfect. Collectively, these teachers strived daily to positively influence the lives of students, but were themselves still learning and growing. Yes, he fit in just fine.

Alex had some extra prep to do before his fifth period, so he gathered his things, saluted his friends with a wave, and strode over to the exit. Turning the corner in the hallway with his eyes planted firmly on the pathway before him, he bumped right into Counselor Kris in route to her office.

> From 2.2.1 – "Teachers honor students when they honor their profession."

After exchanging a few harmless chuckles at this second unfortunate collision, Kris exclaimed, "Well, Mr. Clemmington! Running me over again? I thought football season was over."

"Hey now, a good coach never stops practice."

A pleasant conversation ensued as they walked together toward their respective destinations, both along the north wing of East Crossroads. Upon arriving outside the Counselor Corner, they slowed to a stop. In their pause to part ways, their ears picked up on a small group of unsuspecting students conversing just around the corner.

"How's your speech coming for history?"

"Real well! My mom's been helping me, and Mr. Clemmington gave me a few good pointers when I came to see him after school the other day."

"Yeah, he pulled me in before school last week to give me a little help. I'm so glad he did because I was totally stuck."

"I love how much he's been there to help. I love his class; it's so fun and we learn a ton. Who knew studying about a bunch of dead people could be so cool?"

"Totally. Mr. Clemmington's my favorite teacher. I can't wait until we hit the Civil War next semester."

"I'm sure he'll have something cool planned. He always does."

> From 2.1 – "It behooves teachers to cultivate the relationship necessary to create the environment in which students are willing and eager to follow, thus raising their personal expectations."

Alex shyly looked up at Kris, knowing she had heard it too. She met his gaze, holding it firm with a look of satisfaction and delight. They both stood motionless for a brief moment, lost in the remembrance of Alex's gradual transition from Mr. X. to Mr. Clemmington. When the students' conversation turned to another topic, the two friends broke out in honest, contented laughter.

Then just before they parted, Alex reached in his shirt pocket, flipped a fun-sized KitKat to his mentor, turned on his heel, and took a confident step in the direction of his classroom.

Chapter Three Author's Note

The professional world is full of late night conference calls, profit building strategic plans, and travel cases packed with the full array of business attire. However, the world of public education, though commendable as a whole, sometimes tolerates those who come dressed in jeans and are home by three. All while the product we push, the education of the next generation, is infinitely more important than the sale of, say, vacuum cleaners.

It is natural to gradually regress to the path of least resistance. The persistent pressures of planning, teaching, grading, managing, and organizing can weaken even the strongest among us. (Not to mention committee assignments, faculty meetings, parent conferences, distressed students, distressed colleagues, etc. Indeed, a teacher's job description is near never-ending!). However, we must commit to being the models of what we want our students to become. We must approach our profession in the manner we hope they will one day approach theirs. Would we feel comfortable with a surgeon slicing us open who had the habit of cutting corners and rushing his work?

Alex Clemmington learned the value of a professional approach despite the inherent challenges. He also learned the universal mantra that "you reap what you sow." For years his casual approach had yielded moderate returns, but through his transition he discovered the abundant fruit awaiting those who diligently seek it.

Alex also learned how building professional relationships with his students could improve his classroom culture. His own professionalism set the stage for high expectations while his friendly nature and "Quadruple P" interactions engendered trust that beckoned his students to follow his lead. At first, Alex's transformation necessitated deliberate and conscientious daily decisions to act as he had been taught; however, with time it became habit. His student relations eventually became completely natural, a part of the class culture itself.

The manner in which you, your colleagues, and every other teacher applies the principle of relationships of respect and trust will be different. Though the principle is universal, its most effective application will depend upon the teacher's own strengths and weaknesses, community expectations, and the unique needs of individual students. It is the teacher's duty to tip the balancing act of professionalism and friendliness in the favor of students.

A wise and dedicated teacher is of greater worth to the world than a CEO. Yes, that CEO may supply hundreds of needed jobs to the public, but a teacher supplies the public with hundreds of future CEOs. While many of you possess the qualifications to be CEOs yourselves, it is through your sacrifice, dedication, and professional approach to the teaching profession that tomorrow will be better than today.

Questions to Consider – Your Journal Entry #2

1. *How am I currently approaching my position in a professional manner? In what ways can I improve? (Ideas to Consider – lesson preparation, organization, grading and feedback, dress and grooming, use of instructional time, use of preparation time, interaction with colleagues, willingness to change, etc.)*

2. *How would I define my student interactions? Business-like? Professional yet friendly? Friends? What am I doing well and what methods could I implement to improve?*

3. *What extrinsic motivators have I recently used? Were they needed? How could they have been replaced with intrinsic motivators?*

Chapter Four

Paul and the Principle of Reinforcing the Positive

The halls of East Crossroads were filled with students extra early, it being the first day of school. Like an amusement park, the scene was chaotic. The packed crowd scampered about in a labyrinth of different directions. Some students exhibited apprehension at the prospects of the oncoming ride. Others, well-seasoned, lazed about narcissistically, content to join together in poking fun at the nervous newcomers.

> Reinforcing the Positive – Desired student behavior is reinforced by ignoring inconsequential behavior, recognizing desired behavior, and properly addressing consequential misbehavior.

Apprehensive sixth graders scurried around with schedules in hand, trying to navigate the bustling tangle of hallways before them. Inwardly, they weighed which was the greatest stressor of the moment, avoiding the big kids, locating first period, or figuring out how to infiltrate the impenetrable fortress that was their locker.

The seventh graders wandered around, more worried about locating friends than classes. Yet, it was hard to recognize their once close peers after three summer months that brought four more inches of leg, three more inches of torso, and a disfigured face caught between an influx of both fuzz and pimples.

The eighth graders, in all their grandeur and authority, clumped about in pods of social justice, varying in shape, size, and degrees of clamor. Their time had now arrived, and they intended to kick it off with a bang.

One particular female eighth grade group of three, a little smaller and quieter than most, softly squealed shrieks of delight at their much anticipated reunion. Their dispositions complemented each other nicely. Where one girl was shy, another was outgoing. Where one was lazy, another was diligent. Where one was ditzy, another was bright. This mesh of contrasting personalities strengthened their bond all the more. So, what would naturally be task number one on the first day of school for such a trio of friends?

"Tell me we all have first period PE together!"

"Hee! Yeah! Looks like it!"

"Totally cool! And second period Spanish with Senor Ramirez?"

"Si senorita!"

"What about Language Arts? I have somebody named Ms. Price; she must be new."

"Oh no! I've got Mrs. Livingston."

"And you have Price third period? Darn, I've got her fifth."

"Oh boy, looks like we're in for a long year in language arts. And we all know I won't be in math with you. I'm sure you both made it into Dr. LaValle's advanced math. Right?"

"Yeah. You probably got Mr. Harding."

The excitement of the giddy girls was only somewhat abated at learning that not all their classes were together. The prospects of a promising new year shined bright; well, for now at least.

"You guessed it. Okay now, what about science? I've got Ms. Young seventh period."

"Me too! I've heard she's nice."

The two who had seventh period science together stopped and looked at their friend who was staring at her schedule with an expression of utter horror. It was this particular friend who was known to balance the others' playful nature by her dedication to her studies. She was attentive, thoughtful, and determined. When one visualized her face, the most prominent impression were her studious glasses. Which was curious because she didn't even wear glasses; they just seemed to fit her character.

As the silence persisted, tension increased. It appeared as if her fierce expression was an attempt to either burn the schedule or change reality, either of which would have sufficed.

"Kim, what's wrong? Your face is all red. It's okay if you don't have science seventh period. We still have a few other classes together."

"Yeah Kim, you love science. You'd probably ignore our notes anyway."

Kim looked up from her schedule at her two friends, losing the battle with her fragile tear ducts. She gathered her strength enough to whisper the cause of her dejection.

"It's not that we don't have science together. It's the teacher. I have – Mr. Lowry."

Mr. Paul Lowry sat at his desk, peering menacingly at his students as they silently read from their science textbooks. He eyed them from behind a magazine which covered the old man's face from the nose down. All that could be seen were his excessive forehead wrinkles resting atop his gray, bushy eyebrows. The despot's piercing, reproachful eyes were on perpetual prowl from behind the magazine, searching for any and all signs of student insubordination: notes, doodles, whispers, and other typical adolescent behavior.

This had been a challenging yet exciting week for Paul, challenging because the seats in his class were full of students, and exciting because this was the last year he had to suffer through said occupied seats. For in April, Paul would turn fifty-nine and a half, the age where he could draw on retirement without penalty. He was like an oversized nut trapped in a thick shell, unable to escape its sullen confines to the open air of retirement freedom.

But this was the year he'd finally escape. No more lessons. No more tests. No more students. He had but thirty eight weeks, now thirty seven, to endure.

Paul set down his magazine but remained seated at his desk. "Time's up! Between today's and yesterday's reading, you should have finished chapter one by now. If not, homework. Tomorrow you'll answer the questions at the end of the chapter. This will be closed book, so if you feel the need to study tonight, do it. You'll especially want to review the bolded vocabulary words relating to chemical and physical change."

One student dared to lean over and whisper to a neighbor. "I wish I could physically change right out of this class."

> From 3.4 – "When a teacher attends to a misbehavior, the student received the attention they sought and are therefore more likely to do it again."

Paul's hearing had fortunately retired in his mid-50s, so he didn't hear the comment. However, those spry 20/20 eyes hadn't aged since grade school. He noticed when a page turned or a pencil tip snapped, so he certainly could tell when a student leaned over to whisper to a neighbor.

"You! After class! For that you get to participate in a little table cleaning experiment."

Another student whispered, "An experiment in science class? Now that's an idea."

Paul whipped around, his eyes on the prowl yet unable to make up for his ears' deficiency this time.

Kim sat at a table in the center of the room, hunched low in an effort, she reasoned, to blend in. However, truth be told, merely blending in wasn't her ultimate goal; in reality, she was hiding.

This week had been horrific. Though her other classes brought with them certain challenges, none were quite like seventh period science with Mr. Lowry. He was mean. He was angry. He avoided teaching and student interaction as much as his students avoided him. Ever perched behind his desk, he was like an owl of the night waiting to pounce upon unsuspecting, innocent students who walked slightly off course. His talons were sharp. His beak penetrating. His head grotesquely on a swivel swinging from student to magazine to student. Though just as piercing, Mr. Lowry only lacked the beauty of an owl's large, round eyes.

Empowered

Well, perhaps his were so, only they were hidden behind his abnormally bushy eyebrows.

Paul returned to his desk and again reached for his magazine with a cover depicting a single bowling pin leaning slightly to the side as if resisting the inevitable tumble. Bold, yellow letters across the top of the photo appropriately proclaimed *"OH, SPARE ME!"*

"I expect all A's on tomorrow's chapter quiz. Now, off with you!"

"But Mr. Lowry, the bell hasn't rung yet," shyly questioned a student with a hand in the air.

"Off with you!"

Kim forced herself to the middle of the pack of escaping rodents in flight from the predator. She, rather unknowingly, repeated in her mind, "May, May, May… this spring; just endure."

Glaring at his fleeing prey, Mr. Lowry, quite knowingly, chanted in his mind, "May, May, May… this spring; just endure."

> From 3.2 – Students should feel "encompassed by an environment that is safe, positive, and appreciative of good behavior."

"… So you can see now how my popcorn is popping! The students totally understand my expectations now, just like Kris told me would happen. Now I'll be able to fill my pot with the delicious taste of buttery knowledge!"

Sheri inhaled excessively in an attempt to steady her overgrown enthusiasm, while Mr. Alex Clemmington tried to survive the verbal onslaught. Nearby teachers couldn't help but stop to observe this abnormal monologue from the first year teacher. Some gawked. Others smirked. Mrs. Trisha LaValle's reaction was a cross between a chuckle and a sneer.

Paul, however, could hear no more. He had endured the young little bowling pin mercilessly orate for days about this new school counselor. Her enthusiasm was irritating. Her optimism, annoying. Her positive energy, suffocating. So what, naturally, does darkness do when accosted by light? Fight back. Produce doubt. Induce shadows of comfort for him and discord for her. For after all, misery does love company.

"Bravo kid. Now the real trick is to make those urchins do the same tomorrow. Harder than it seems. Good luck with that pile of bowling balls."

Sheri stalled, her momentum thwarted by this unanticipated strike. Unable to hide this small rip in her tapestry of confidence, Paul pounced to seize advantage of her now evident weakness.

"Those students can't succeed in your class, or any other! It's just the sad tale of the middle school years; students come lost in the transition of their own bodies. The best you can do is just to help them survive. Some may come out of it one day in high school or later on. Just survive; that's all you can do."

To his great satisfaction, Sheri left lunch that day with heavier shoulders than when she had entered. Feeling smug, Paul was anxious to sit back and observe the effects of the shadow he had cast. Yet as the days passed, Sheri exemplified resilience and persistence. Bouncing back from the doubt planted by Paul and later confirmed by her students, Sheri began to find success. And with success, for an enthusiast like Sheri, came great animation.

With each passing day the walls of the teachers' lounge echoed with Sheri's orations. Though always careful to keep a distance from her previous attacker, Sheri could not restrain her audio discharges from permeating the lounge at large. And while many of her colleagues learned to enjoy her youthful enthusiasm, the shadow in the corner felt nauseated with displeasure.

Her enthusiasm was his aggravation, and her passion was his exasperation. This talk of one Counselor Kris persisted for days on end. The more Sheri talked of her, the more Paul resented her. The more glowing light that was shed upon this mere mortal, the more Paul reveled in the shadow it created for himself.

Kris. Counselor Kris. Paul barely knew her. He'd rarely ever seen her let alone spoken with her. Yet, he didn't like her. He didn't like what she seemed to stand for. He didn't like the effects she had on others. Her supposed improvements threatened his reign. The light she provided diminished his own ominous influence. He wanted none of it. Yes, Paul resolutely concluded he wanted nothing to do with this Counselor Kris.

Or did he?

Kim sat silently at her table, huddled over her science textbook in her usual effort to camouflage herself. Today's class was no different from most others. Students silently read from their textbook in feigned preparation for an upcoming chapter quiz while their teacher settled behind his desk near the front of class, one eye perusing his bowling magazine and the other searching for misbehavior. And inevitably each day, some brave – or perhaps reckless – student dared to whisper or pass a note or breathe. Each time they were sure to be picked off by a verbal onslaught that was as demeaning as it was inaccurate.

> From 3.3 – "Though you may win the battle by temporarily stopping [inconsequential] behaviors, you lose the overall war of creating a culture of success, so choose your battles wisely."

The man simply had trained himself to always aim for a strike.

Kim instinctively turned at the creak of the classroom door to see the gangly form of the assistant principal, Mr. Phippen, with a note in hand, apparently there to deliver a message to her teacher. Upon taking a few moments to stand in the doorframe to observe the class, he soon spied Mr. Lowry behind his magazine. Kim kept hidden watch as Mr. Phippen glided upon his stork legs to the teacher's desk where Mr. Lowry continued perusing his fine literature. Kim noticed her classmates also abandon their reading, unable to stop themselves from observing the lamb approaching the lion.

Mr. Phippen leaned over and whispered to the man behind the magazine, "Mr. Lowry."

Met with silence, he tried again, "Mr. Lowry."

Nothing. So, Mr. Phippen cautiously put his hand on the teacher's shoulder and breathed, "Hey, Paul."

Mr. Lowry inhaled deeply, closed his magazine with his finger marking his spot, and glared up at the twig standing before him. Kim was surprised to see Mr. Lowry's reaction stop there. After a few uncomfortable seconds of the carnivore sizing up his gangly prey, he withdrew his stare and returned to his magazine, apparently concluding that a kill of so little meat wasn't worth the effort.

Kim then determined that her assistant principal must be either dangerously naïve or simply senseless, for he gripped the magazine, pulled it from her teacher's paws, and placed it, closed, atop his desk. She and her classmates gasped in horror at such an error in judgment. And yet, Mr. Phippen didn't stop there. He all but cast himself into the jaws of his predator by leaning over the magazine and declaring in quiet confidence, "Paul, there are better times for pleasure reading."

The students instinctively recoiled at the onslaught sure to come. As one might do just before the climax of a horror movie, some covered their heads. Others their ears. One shy boy in the corner actually crawled under a table.

Mr. Lowry slowly raised his head, surprise and anger shooting from his reproachful eyes. The gray from his bushy brows accentuated the blackness of his stare. The bully then rose to his feet and remained locked in the intimidating glare he had perfected by terrifying scores of students over the years.

All held their breath. The air was tense. Mr. Phippen buckled slightly under the pressure and yielded just enough to glance aside and scan the class. The students' unnerving reactions revealed to the poor dupe the foolishness of his persistence.

Now more shrunken than his previous naivety would allow, Mr. Phippen feebly returned his eyes to the enraged glare of Mr. Lowry. Clearly defeated, Kim's valiant yet imprudent assistant principal then bowed his head in submission. "We can, um, continue talking... uh, discussing this, another time... uh, later."

The lamb then turned tail and fled to the exit.

Kim watched Mr. Lowry sit back down with an air of victorious satisfaction. He looked over the room with a sinister smile so every student fully understood who was really in charge. Once satisfied with his accomplishments, he snatched up his magazine, flipped to his previous page, and returned to his routine as if nothing ever happened.

Negative emotion is a cyclical trap. When one sets foot in its lengthy snare, the emotions of envy, blame, and pessimism swirl together in a cacophony of binding restraint. It's often slow, subtle even. Yet when left unguarded, negativity envelops its victim in a suffocating haze.

However, just beyond the tempest is the refreshing gleam of sunshine, enticing effort to push through the clouds. While some may have strength enough to pull themselves up from the muck of their own accord, others may not be able to alone. Like a storm-tossed boat lost in the clenches of a turbulent sea, their best chance of escape is a benevolent rescuer to come and guide them to safety. Indeed, they need a willing benefactor.

Things hadn't changed for weeks. The pattern in science class continued to be silent reading intermixed with occasional retaliatory outbursts from Mr. Lowry from behind his desk and magazine. Kim had concluded there was no hope. This was to be her fate for the duration of the year: textbooks, quizzes, bowling, and shouting.

And today had been like all the others. Kim concealed herself as best she could, more concerned about avoiding the storm cloud in the corner than actually learning

> From 3.2 – "Student success is more likely to be achieved when the classroom culture is such that students *want* to behave appropriately."

science. And the cloud himself again seemed content to enjoy the benefits of his intimidation and in wasting away another day as he inched closer to retirement.

The rigid silence broke with an innocuous creak. Surprised, Kim shifted just enough to identify the cause of the disruption. There, in the open doorframe, stood the new school counselor, note in hand, apparently in need of a quick chat with the teacher. Kim hadn't had much interaction with the school counselor, but she had taken notice of her pleasant demeanor. Kim had been drawn to her bright smile, strong step, and welcoming countenance. And there she stood, in stark contrast to the gloom at the opposite end of the room.

Immersed in his reading, Mr. Lowry had yet to notice his visitor. What Kim did not know was that Mr. Lowry had also taken special notice of the new counselor. Ms. Price's accolades about Kris had first annoyed the old man, even pushing him to resentment. Yet, when that goofy football coach made mention of what Kris was doing for him, Mr. Lowry finally acknowledged what he had theretofore suppressed – intrigue.

Paul had begun to observe her, well, from a distance of course; he had a reputation to maintain after all. And make no mistake, Kris's optimism and upbeat nature rubbed him as badly as text message grammar to an English teacher. And yet he couldn't help but be drawn in. Was it her newness? Was it her influence? Was it how the lounge conversation always seemed to come back to her even though she herself was rarely present? Whatever the reason, Paul was interested. And as time passed and Kris's influence swelled, so did his concealed fascination.

As Kris hovered momentarily in the doorframe striving to locate the teacher, which of course was more challenging when he's hiding behind a desk and magazine, Kim couldn't help but recall that unfortunate confrontation with Mr. Phippen just days earlier. She silently shuddered, fearing that a similar fate now awaited her teacher's next victim. Except this victim, to Kim, was much more than an innocent lamb. Here stood an eagle, bold and beautiful, unknowingly entering an inevitable trap.

Kim quivered again, this time unable to hide the motion. Mr. Lowry's vigilant eye detected the movement. With no more notice than his intake of breath, Kim recoiled at the oncoming attack.

"You! A note!"

"Mr. Lowry, no," Kim backpedaled. "I was reading and just got the shivers."

"Yeah, right. I haven't been a teacher twice as long as you've been alive without learning your tricks."

"Yeah, but..." stammered Kim.

"...well 'yabba dabba doo' to you too. Stop stuttering and hand it over. Let's find out the latest teenage gossip."

> From 3.5.1 – "Address the [misbehavior] as privately as possible... [to] maintain the student's dignity."

Having yet to be noticed by the all-searching eye, Counselor Kris took two steps into the room. Paul instantly stopped. His jaw ajar and his eyes stunned at the appearance of this unexpected visitor, for the first time in Kim's eighth grade experience, Mr. Lowry was speechless. It appeared as if his own trap had closed in on him. Somehow, someway, with merely her presence, this woman had reduced Kim's teacher to a shell of his habitual choleric persona.

Dazed and disoriented, Mr. Lowry's eyes mechanically followed Kris's smooth approach. Kim and her classmates, stupefied by this uncharacteristic turn of events, watched with great surprise as Kris handed Mr. Lowry the note she had brought, whispered a kind word in his ear, smiled, and happily retreated out the door.

Mr. Lowry remained standing for a few moments longer. Then, with a shake of his head, he gazed over the class with a sheepish look and returned to his seat, without so much as looking at the still-open magazine.

—m—

"Nice job, Cathy! I've got several students that come to me right from your class, and all they can talk about is their projects. They can't get enough!" One middle aged teacher slurped up a noodle and offered a deserving compliment to her colleague who was just sitting down for her midday meal.

"I know! It's so exciting to see how much they've perked up since August. I hope our fun isn't interrupting your class."

> From 4.2.3 – Student-centered teachers "are team players amongst faculty members, able and willing to share and sacrifice for the good of the whole."

"Of course not. In fact, I've found that the enthusiasm they bring from yours carries over to mine. It's helped raise our standards a bit too."

A third voice joined the conversation, "You two have really led the way with this group of kids this year. It's been fun to sit back and observe their growth. I can't help but be amazed at their collective change in attitude."

And then a fourth, "I think we've all been trying to raise the bar a bit. It's been fun to see what high expectations coupled with some smiles can do."

Paul silently sipped his lukewarm tomato soup at the corner table of the teachers' lounge. He never looked up at the flurry of positive energy before him, yet he absorbed every word. He'd observed how over time the dynamics of the lounge had shifted. A new tune began to brew, and as it strengthened, his weakened. Ms. Sheri Price, of course, was the first and loudest of the bunch, but she was soon joined by others. One by one, the effects of professionalism and optimism seeped deeper and wider. Indeed, things were shifting; the culture was shifting. And though her presence in the lounge was scarce, Paul knew the instigator of it all.

Kris.

Day after day, Paul sat back intently observing and feebly resisting the lure of this positive culture shift. From his self-imposed shadows, Paul noticed his own feelings evolve from initial contempt, to forced indifference, and now thorough intrigue. Knowing what was next in the natural sequence, and understanding how utterly contrary it was to the person he'd become, he furiously fought that inner battle. He felt it coming. He felt *desire* marching forth. And yet still, he suppressed it, determined to stifle its steady advance.

"To arms!" he silently cried. "Rally the troops! Reinforce the blockade!"

He lost.

He lost miserably. In seeing all the positive change around him, Paul couldn't help but notice that he, Mr. Paul Lowry, now stuck out like bumpers at the Saturday morning bowling league. He no longer belonged. He was abandoned to his own reclusion. His darkness used to blend in nicely with the gray of mediocrity around him, but as the gray lightened, his darkness appeared bolder. And as the sun has power to burn off lingering storm clouds, so had this positive culture shift at East Crossroads. He felt the stirring and the longing. He felt the tug of optimism pulling his storm-tossed boat to the safety of the shore.

Conflicted, Paul eventually concluded that he had two options. First, he could waste away in his own little corner, seeking refuge until retirement in his self-imposed shell of dissatisfaction. Or second, he could open up. He could grab hold of the line pulling him in and save himself with positive change. The former proved easy yet woeful; the latter appeared challenging yet rewarding.

Still unwilling to completely surrender, Paul eventually concluded he'd at least confront this temptress, this instigator of change. He'd go and find out for himself how this Counselor Kris seemed to wield so much influence. And then, having gained such usable knowledge, he'd be better equipped to determine his course.

Paul forced a sinister grin as he marched to the Counselor Corner. On the surface, he tried to convince himself that he'd crush this little ray of sunshine as he'd done others over the years. And yet this forced façade couldn't fully mask his inner trepidation; his gloom now marched to its doom.

Kris, upon noticing the dark figure silhouetted in the doorway of her office, exclaimed, "Well, it's Mr. Paul Lowry himself! What a pleasure to see you this afternoon. Please, please, come in!"

Paul, somewhat hesitantly, found his way to one of the empty white leather chairs opposite the small wooden table with the candy dish on top. Feeling the need to convey the reason for his unannounced visit, Paul tripped over his words as if he'd forgotten to tie his bowling shoes and tied his tongue instead. "I, uh… You know… I… the other day…"

Noticing Paul's discomfort, Kris interrupted to save him from himself. "You know Paul, I've been thinking a lot about you since my brief visit to your class last week."

Paul frowned, assuming an oncoming reproach. "Oh, is that so?" he sneered.

Kris continued with an amiable tone that meant, to the pessimist Paul anyway, that she must be setting him up. "Well, yes. I couldn't help but wonder what gems of wisdom you must have from your years of experience. I understand you've been teaching science for decades! How wonderful! I can only imagine the number of students you've influenced and tricks of the trade you've learned that really only come with experience."

Paul sat a little taller, but still felt unsure of Kris's motives. "Well, you know, you certainly pick up a few things over time."

Kris reached into the drawer of the table separating the two, pulled out a couple of KitKats, and tossed one Paul's way. Being on watchful guard, he snatched the candy bar out of the air with the agility of one whose primary sport is anything but bowling. Unwrapping her own, Kris continued.

"Now, forgive me for the friendly accusation, but you've been selfish young man! I know myself and many others in this school would love to take advantage of your knowledge. Sharing, you know, doesn't take away from what you have; it makes it greater."

Paul buckled under the barrage of compliments. He wasn't used to receiving such treatment, and certainly not giving it. Positive talk had, over the years, become foreign to him. But he liked it; his ego was stroked. Without full realization, Paul's inner-self opened up ever so slightly.

"Well, you know," Paul stammered, "I'd like to say I know my stuff. Yet, I've kind of trended toward keeping to myself as I've grown older. Perhaps I've isolated myself a bit much."

Kris interrupted with the encouraging smile of a close confidant. "In your isolation you've kept those pearls to yourself! Now, shame on you Mr. Lowry! Isn't Thanksgiving more enjoyable when you share it with others? We may need to have a little chat about this. I'm sure your feast is divine, and I expect an invitation!"

The two enjoyed a hearty chuckle together, and Kris tossed Paul another KitKat.

Paul's once formidable barricade against his optimistic enemy had become severely breached. Kris was now able to penetrate with ease through a variety of weakened holes, the most gaping of which now became evident to this benevolent attacker – remembrance. She pounced.

"So, tell me Paul, exactly how long have you been teaching?"

In an effort to conceal his poor manners, Paul mumbled as he spoke with a mouth full of chocolate. "Twenty nine. This is my twenty ninth year."

"How old are you now?"

Paul, feeling safe, didn't hesitate to respond to the personal questioning. "I just turned fifty nine."

"Wow. So that means that by the end of the year you'll have been a teacher as long as you haven't. Half of your life – that's amazing! And next year you'll be able to say you've been a teacher for three decades, and you've spent more than half of your life in the service of students. How incredible!"

"Well, that's not entirely true," responded Paul with an embarrassed shrug. "This is my last year. I plan to retire in May."

Shocked, Kris dropped her candy bar. "Retire? At fifty nine? You're still so young!" Paul looked down and fell silent, feeling a twinge of guilt at the thought of leaving on what he was now discovering were bad terms.

Kris recovered from a few moments of silent thought and replied with an encouraging smile. "Well Paul, I suppose after nearly thirty years of quality service to others, impressionable youth of all people, you deserve a little time for yourself. Good for you. My only regret is not having enough time to learn from your experience. But hey, that still leaves me a few months, right?"

Paul nodded in reply and flashed an awkward smile. After another moment of quiet contemplation, Kris inquired, "Paul, what were your first few years of teaching like?"

A small snicker escaped his morose visage. "Boy, it's been a while since I thought of those days. But yeah, I started teaching on the west side of town over at Plainview Middle School. That building has long since been demolished; even then it was old."

"Do you remember your classes?" proceeded Kris carefully. "Any students?"

Paul's gaze lofted past his questioner, and he let his mind waft back to his carefully hidden memories. Back he went, past the textbooks, past the chapter quizzes, past the bowling, and even past East Crossroads. His mind eventually caught hold of the memory of his first seventh grade science class. His stern face softened, revealing delight at the memory.

"My first year, ha! Boy, was I terrible. I had no idea what I was doing. I think I eventually lost count of the number of beakers and test tubes I broke. After a while it became quite the joke with my students. I remember one particular class made up with their own little cheer each time I broke one – something like, 'crash, bang, booooom.' They got so good they'd do it in unison on the spot, and then of course they'd help me clean up the mess. What a fun group."

The two enjoyed twenty minutes more of Paul's divergence from the bowling lane to memory lane. For the most part Kris kept quiet, offering only a comment here and a question there. She instead sat back and watched Paul's eyes light up as he rehearsed story after story of those pleasant teaching memories, some funny, some serious, yet all recalling pleasant interactions with the students of his past.

The gradual change in Paul's countenance was dramatic. Yes, his eyebrows were still bushy, but they now angled outward in an expression of contentment. Yes, his forehead was still wrinkled, but now it softened to a grandfatherly state. There sat Mr. Paul Lowry, uncharacteristically devoid of resentment, blame, and victimization. His previous robust defenses against the positive in the world had waned. Once eager, now meager, the barricade defending his state of pessimism had given way, given way to the bliss of remembrance.

Paul sprang through the front doors of East Crossroads the following morning with a bounce in his step. A willing smile graced his face in a manner that was as rare as it was awkward. The result of the attempted smile resembled that of the stumbling Mr. Phippen striving to orate a motivational speech at faculty meeting, misplaced and downright clumsy. But the effort was sincere!

Paul rounded the corner past the front office, still sporting the upside down version of his face. A few teachers passed by along the other side of the hall, as was their habit. In route, Mr. Clemmington caught sight of Paul's facial contortions, causing an involuntary double take.

Yet taking no notice, Paul hopped along past the library from where Ms. Sheri Price was exiting. In passing, Paul bellowed a jolly "good morning," and it only took Sheri a respectable five seconds to pick her jaw off the ground.

He then, on the way to his classroom, coasted through the math wing where he spotted Dr. LaValle writing the day's homework on the whiteboard just outside her room. Skipping by he said, "Hi there, Trish-a! Lookin' good today. The curls are a nice change of pace from the bun."

Trisha was unusually tongue-tied, surprised at the sight of his jack-o-lantern grin. His extra facial wrinkles, like the ripples of a withering pumpkin, caused Trisha to bite her tongue.

Paul then bounded into his classroom, eager to greet his students. Soon thereafter the first period bell sounded while he was wrapping up some morning preparations. As usual, his students silently and reluctantly crept to their seats, pulled out their textbooks, and plunged into their habitual methods of self-defense.

Upon finishing his work, Paul stood up and skipped to the front, flashing his heretofore unseen faded-yellow stumps. "Good morning class. It's a pleasure to see you today."

A noiseless current moved throughout the students. Caught off guard by the friendly reception, their suspicion and anxiety increased. They were unwilling to take what they thought was their temperamental teacher's bait, so they remained still.

Undaunted, Paul continued. "Today I was hoping to start with something a little different. James, can you bring me that graduated cylinder on the counter behind you?"

All eyes spun around to their targeted classmate, horrified at the prospects. James imploringly searched for aid amongst his peers. No one dared move. Frozen in indecision, James remained seated having concluded that the consequences of inaction would likely be less painful than the consequences of misaction.

Paul prodded James and his peers another time or two, searching for anything in return. Instead, the deafening silence rang loud and clear; his prisoners would not leave their cell, even when set free. This realization broke Paul's spirits. Like a broken blister on his bowling hand, it popped. He popped. His graceless grin fell to a grimace while his eyebrows turned inward, his forehead wrinkles protruded, and the flash in his eyes warned of forthcoming retribution.

> From 3.5 – "The moment misbehaviors are addressed is significant. Addressing the student improperly may cause harm."

The students took cover behind the thick defenses of their textbooks at the onslaught of their teacher's verbal lashings. Carrying on way beyond his usual tirades, Mr. Lowry subjected his students to a series of accusations, threats, and "why do I try's." His pleasantries had been replaced with poison.

Eventually, Paul sighed, sulked his way to his desk, and plopped down his deflated frame. Only when he reached for his bowling magazine did the students finally relax. Their lives had achieved normalcy again. Mr. Lowry's five minute attempt at kindness had vanished as quickly as it had come.

"It's ridiculous; just flat out absurd."

"It's absurd that your students would be a little resistant to change?"

"No! It's absurd that my students would treat me with such disrespect, especially after my cheery welcoming to class! What an ungrateful group of misfit teens. In my day, no student would ever..."

Paul's fuming from the "mistreatment" had only strengthened with each subsequent class. Though he hadn't attempted the same warm reception after first period, each passing student was like another log on his internal fire. Unknowingly, first period struck the match while each ensuing class fueled the flames. And the lot now fell to Kris to tame the blaze before her.

Her strategy? Listen and wait for it to burn down. For she knew that an attempt to douse the fire with reason or suggestions might actually spark its resurgence. No, better let the anger gradually consume itself.

So, for quite some time Kris gave no more than an occasional nod of the head. Paul's ranting seemed to vacillate from extreme to moderate, raging to fair, a ten to a seven and back again. Yet, over time, the peaks seemed less high and the drops a little lower. The ups and downs of the wildfire were subsiding as Paul burned through the needed fuel to sustain the intensity. Eventually, Paul's rage had reduced itself to no more than a smoldering heap of black ash, silent and beaten. The fire was gone, yes, but what remained didn't seem much more promising.

Kind and gentle, Kris slowly reached her hand across the table and deposited an offering. She waited for Paul to make a move. With his head in his hands, he spied the gift from between his fingers. It was a fun-sized KitKat bar. This simple act of fellowship produced a softening effect throughout Paul's smoldering psyche. It reminded him of the feelings he had that morning, the feelings of newness and cheerfulness brought on by his new found confidant. No, Kris wasn't giving him a candy bar; she was giving him friendship.

Paul reached for the gift, swallowing both the candy and his pride.

Soon, he drew in a deep breath and made a request that epitomized his new desire to be the teacher he once was.

"Kris, will you help me?"

Kris's countenance spoke volumes before she even uttered a response. Smiling empathetically, she chose her words wisely, wanting to make the most of this tender moment, this crossroads in the career of her colleague and the students he served.

"Yes."

"Did you see Paul this morning?" Sheri asked Alex at lunch that day.

"Yeah! It was crazy," he answered. "He was, like, actually… smiling."

"He even wished me a 'good morning.' I don't think I've ever seen him so friendly."

"Doom and gloom, that's all he's ever been. I wonder what happened. He must have either scored big in the stock market or finally bowled a perfect 300."

Trisha interrupted the pair's conversation from her neighboring table, relishing the opportunity to spread the juicy news she'd heard from some of her second period students. "Well, the old grump couldn't keep it up that long. I heard that within a few minutes of class, he completely blew up. Kids weren't responding, so his pasted on smile gave way to the usual ogre."

"Oh my!" Sheri covered her mouth at the visual.

"Yep," retorted Trisha with a sinister sneer. "An old dog just can't learn new tricks."

Later that week, Paul followed through on his inner commitment and joined Kris in her office, where she was following through on hers. And while the old man came willing to learn, the years of bad habits had encircled his inner goodness with a thick outer shell, testing Kris's endurance to work through the hardened coconut to locate the nutrition within. Simply put, Paul was a tough nut to crack.

"You see Paul, the ultimate objective is to create a classroom environment in which your students are most likely to succeed. You can't force success. You can't even force good behavior. But you can, however, create a culture in your class where students will want to succeed and behave of their own accord."

"What are you talking about?" Paul argued. "I've forced good behavior for years! My kids never talk out of turn. No notes. No whispers. They're straight laced and straight arrowed."

"Good point," Kris replied. "However, I think it depends on your definition of 'good' behavior. What do you think; does good just mean, 'not bad?'"

"Well, no. I guess not."

"Okay, so what else might 'good' behavior be?"

"I suppose it means doing good things as well, like following directions, participating, and asking questions."

"Great!" Kris commended. "Now, let me ask another question. Have your students been following directions, participating, and asking questions? They certainly haven't been 'bad,' but have they been 'good?'"

Paul responded with an affirmative grunt, knowing full well what kind of culture he had created.

Kris noted the reaction and continued on before he had a chance to backpedal. "Okay now, how would you define the term 'success'?"

Paul took a few moments to gather his thoughts. "Perhaps, accomplishing something worthwhile that makes you stretch, something that makes you proud."

"I couldn't have defined it any better myself! Now, think back over the course of this year. Tell me a success your students have accomplished."

Paul's mind reached back to August and scanned forward to the present. All he could recall were textbooks, quizzes, and a fair amount of yelling. He was about to say how many of his students achieved good grades on their chapter quizzes, but he caught himself before giving Kris the chance to do so. That wasn't real success. In the end, memorizing information for a single quiz only to forget it all the moment the paper was handed in, certainly could not be defined as success. It wasn't something worthwhile or something of which to be proud.

Now feeling a little picked on, Paul dropped his head. He had come to the realization that he had failed at a teacher's singular goal: helping students succeed. It stung. Their lack of success was his failure. Kris sensed Paul's silent conclusion, so before he sunk too low, she intervened.

"Now, it's not entirely your fault. You cannot force failure just as you cannot force success. The world is full of incredible stories of individuals overcoming daunting circumstances to achieve great things. Success is a choice, a choice every individual has the capacity to make."

"True," Paul interjected, "but how many more failures in the world could have instead been successes under different circumstances?"

"Exactly! You're exactly right! And that brings us back to the ultimate objective of a teacher, to create an environment most conducive to student success. It is our job as educators to create circumstances that encourage students to actually choose the path of success for themselves."

Paul sat up a little straighter, and his face grew a little lighter. "Good. Yes. But one question still looms. How?"

"Perfect question. Let's start that discussion with a little analogy."

Kris pulled out a blank sheet of paper and a pencil. With the paper on the table between them, she drew the beginnings of a simple diagram, starting with a single horizontal line stretching across the width of the page.

Kris questioned, "Have you ever spent much time at the beach?"

"It's been a while," chuckled Paul. "Not many would enjoy seeing this unfortunate case of 'old man syndrome' I've come down with lately."

Reciprocating with a hearty laugh, Kris continued. "Well, as a kid I spent a lot of time at the beach. One of our favorite things to do was to build, what we called, a sand fortress. We really weren't into the castle thing, but we loved creating a network of pools connected together by streams winding around the mountains formed from the remains of digging out the holes. We called it our family fortress. Each of us dug our own pool to the size and depth we wanted, but we were all connected together by the pathways."

Kris erased the middle half of the horizontal line on the paper and reconnected the now two lines with a concave semicircle dipping beneath the previous surface, clearly depicting one of the holes of the sand fortress Kris had described.

"Sounds fun, fun and ambitious," Paul said while popping in a fruity candy. "I'd probably just have sat under an umbrella snacking on chips."

"Ambitious is right. The challenge was that we couldn't just create the fortress and enjoy it the rest of the day. Whenever we poured in water, it would slowly tear down the sand walls. It would soak through any crevices in the sand then drag the walls to the bottom of the hole." Kris then shaded the sides of the hole in her diagram. She also shaded up from the bottom, indicating how the water pulled the sand from the walls to the base.

Kris continued, "We soon learned that if we wanted our fortress to last, we had to be constantly vigilant. We had to dig out the bottom, build up the walls, and regularly replenish the lost water that seeped into the sand."

Paul responded with a look of bewilderment, raising his bushy eyebrows to the point of concealing half of his wrinkled forehead. Kris caught his signal of confusion, so she spelled it out plainly. "Paul, if you want to create a culture of success in your class, you've got to do the same as the sand fortress. The water represents your students' success. The hole represents the culture of success you create for them. The deeper and wider the hole, the greater the capacity for success. And yet, each time you pour in a bucket of water…"

"…sand from the walls is washed to the bottom," interrupted Paul, catching on.

"Making your hole a little smaller."

"So what you're saying is that creating a culture of success isn't just a one-time deal. It needs regular maintenance and attention."

Kris leaned back in her chair, pleased at their progress. They seemed to have stripped through the outer layer of Paul's shell. "Precisely. And yet, as a child, I noticed something peculiar about the hole. If we gave it the attention it needed at the beginning, over the course of the day it would need less and less maintenance. You're the science teacher, so perhaps you could better explain the reasons, but it seemed that the sand would develop some sort of hardening quality that would better hold the water. It could certainly be easily disturbed if punctured, but when left alone, it remained pretty firm. At that point we didn't have to conduct constant repairs, just check in periodically and beware to not ruin it."

"So building a classroom culture takes a lot of time and effort up front, but you can enjoy the benefits afterwards with minimal upkeep. Sounds logical."

"What do you say, Paul? Are you up for playing in the sand?"

"I was always more of an indoor guy."

Journal Entry – October 2

What am I, a fourteen year old girl who is too shy to say hello to the cute football player? "Dear Diary, I'm writing to you because I'm too scared to talk out loud…" Bah!

Yet here I am, writing a journal. It's a good thing for Kris that I trust her, or I might have laughed her right out of her own office at the suggestion of a journal. But she sure has shown a way to get me to look at things differently. It's pretty clear now that I let my original good intentions of being a teacher become lost over time. I guess since I never learned how to create a culture of success, students behaved according to whatever culture they wanted, which of course was a culture I didn't like. I then let that frustration burn and fester until I became this old grump.

No more. I can do better. I can't control my students, but I can control myself.

So, Kris gave me an assignment to add a little more detail to her sand fortress analogy (Really? A writing assignment?). She asked me to match elements of the analogy to their interpretation and identify the element on which I most need to work. (What am I, a second grader?) So without further ado… (Catch the sarcasm?).

Depth of Hole = High Expectations. *The higher the expectations, the deeper the hole, and therefore the greater the amount of success that can fit inside.*

Walls Inside Hole = Reinforcing the Positive. *This is what holds the water in its proper place. With regular attention, this solidifies the stability of the hole over time.*

Additional Walls above Hole = Relationships of Respect and Trust. *These relationships bring protection from outside influences and increase the capacity of water inside.*

Pouring in Water = Student-Centered Instruction. *The hole itself does nothing for the student unless filled with a measured amount of student success. The mechanism to fill the hole with as much water as possible is instruction centered on individual student needs.*

My Biggest Need = Reinforcing the Positive. *She didn't allow me to choose all four, so I've dutifully conformed and chosen the obvious. I've been anything but positive, and I know I'll have a hard time getting rid of my negative habits. (Perhaps I could start by not complaining about this journal!)*

Kim looked around the science room, momentarily removing herself from the group experiment to observe the day's odd changes. There was noise, there was movement, and there were smiles, actual smiles!

Mr. Lowry was again trying something new. Last week when he deviated from his habitual read-write-and-yell routine, it didn't last more than five minutes before he made like an acid/base reaction and exploded. With that memory fresh and ripe, Kim and her classmates hadn't been too anxious to play with the chemicals again. Yet Mr. Lowry persisted, and now fifteen minutes in, he'd already broke his long standing record… he'd actually smiled three times!

Yet Kim still had her suspicions, so she kept up her guard. She noticed, however, that many of her classmates were becoming a little too comfortable. One group of boys, in particular, dared to raise their voices above a throaty whisper. "Flirting with flames," Kim thought to herself.

The group assignment had been to conduct an experiment on force and motion. Groups were to roll a toy car with a marble resting in the open seat down a track inclined at varying degrees until it met a wood block impediment that stopped the car and launched the marble. The goal was to see how varying inclines affected the distance of the marble's flight.

Meanwhile, as Kim gazed about, she could see how her classmates were simultaneously conducting another similar experiment, one that held greater personal significance. And this too was an experiment of force and motion: Which student behavioral force would set the teacher in motion? Tapping a pencil. Speaking above a whisper. Looking at another group. And heaven forbid, laughing!

Kim noticed how each student force did indeed yield a Mr. Lowry motion. Yet the two experiments seemed to produce conflicting results. The marble acted according to predictable laws of physics, the greater the incline, the greater the flight distance. Mr. Lowry, however, had no set pattern. While some whispering he shushed, others he didn't. Where he gave the evil eye to some pencil tappers, to others he didn't. Where at times he reminded the whole class to quiet down, at other times he didn't. To Kim, there seemed to be no rhyme or reason to his reactions, no consistency at all. How could they know how much force to use when the motion was different every time?

> From 3.3 – "Harping on every little whisper and pencil tap creates a sense of authoritarianism and may actually reinforce the very behavior you're striving to eliminate."

Despite the class's failure to draw clear conclusions to their prime experiment, Kim was, however, able to add four worthwhile observations to her mental scientific journal. First, Mr. Lowry was trying. Whatever the reason was, the irritable Mr. Lowry was making an effort to actually teach. Second, though he was trying, he had no clue what he was doing. Third, since he had no clue what he was doing, it wasn't working very well. And fourth, since it wasn't working very well, he was starting to get frustrated.

Kim watched her teacher wring his hands and pace the floor. Forehead wrinkles were retaking their place atop his brow. His eyes clouded over with the familiar veil of anger. He was trying to suppress the ogre they'd known for months, but the beast was quickly working its way to the surface. Kim could see the acids and bases mixing, so she clutched her desk in self-preservation at the oncoming explosive reaction.

Yet mercifully, the bell rang. They had done it; they had escaped him. He had done it; he had escaped himself. Mr. Lowry, her grumpy old science teacher, had actually taught a lesson… without exploding!

"I know. I know! It takes time!" Paul slumped over in Kris's office after a tiring day of actual teaching. "It was the first time I poured any water in the fortress, so the walls are going to cave somewhat. But split me some pins! That took more patience than Friday night cosmic bowling surrounded by flirty teenagers!"

Kris's face softened with an encouraging smile. "But you did it. You did it, Paul. That's a big first step. And we haven't even begun discussing strengthening those interior walls by reinforcing the positive. Quite frankly, I'm impressed."

"Impressed my eyeballs are still in their sockets despite all that pressure in my head?" Paul's sarcasm was laced with a tone of satisfaction, for he knew that he had done well, something his pessimistic pride found challenging to admit.

At Paul's joke, Kris let loose a genuine, raucous laugh that penetrated the thick frustrated front sitting before her. The laugh seemed to validate Paul's frustrations and compliment his actions. He sat back, his tense muscles relaxing. At that moment, Kris's laughter was better than any speech she could have given.

After the moment died down, and she could take a deep breath, Kris inquired, "Paul, how do you think your students feel about you? I mean, if they talked to their friends about you, what do you think they'd say?"

"Probably that I'm mean and negative."

"Are you?"

"That's what I'm trying to work on."

"Why have you been negative in the past?"

"Their misbehavior. When they don't follow my rules it sets me off."

"Okay, so why do you think they sometimes don't follow your rules?"

Paul took a moment to come up with an adequate response. His brain returned a gutter ball, so he settled for some juvenile blame. "I don't know. They're teenagers; that's what they do. They test their limits. They bend the rules. It's, like, in their DNA or something."

"Interesting. Do they misbehave in other classes? Have you observed Ms. Price or Dr. LaValle's classes lately?"

"You're kidding, right? I walk on the other side of the hallway when passing the door of our high and mighty Little Miss Trish."

"Well, if you did, you'd see the exact same misbehaving students from your science class fully engaged, diligently working, and behaving properly. Same students, different results."

Paul sat back in the white leather chair and slumped to the side as if he'd taken a jab to the gut. "Now that was low. What's your point, Kris?"

Kris ignored his reaction because she knew that her comment had gotten his full attention. "My point is that behavior is often a product of environment. This is a classic case of The Negativity Trap. You're negative because they're negative to you. They're negative to you because you're negative to them. Then you're even more negative to them, and so forth. It's a cyclical blame game that breeds anger and stifles success.

"So, who was negative first?" Kris continued. "Who was negative second? Well, what came first, the chicken or the egg? Quite frankly, who cares? Let's have steak! What does it matter how it started? Break the cycle, Paul. You're the adult teacher who can control your own emotions and actions. Be the instigator of a new cycle, a cycle that nurtures unity and fosters success."

> From 3.4.2 –
> "Purposefully and dutifully develop the habit of speaking positively with students."

Paul's intent yet puzzled look silently asked the timely question, how?

"Sounds good, but how is it done?" Kris's rhetorical question momentarily hung in silence. "How can you reinforce the interior walls of your sand fortress? Simply put, reinforcing the positive. Just as you've been trapped in a cycle of negativity, human nature works the same way inversely. You be consistently positive to your students, and they'll be positive back to you. And the cycle continues.

"In all my experience, both in my own classroom and in the role of helping others, I have seen this principle to be true. The degrees may vary. The time length may vary. But if you manage students by reinforcing the positive in a consistent manner with the other principles of culture creating, the class at large will reciprocate the actions. The positive cycle will take hold, and you will be able to focus on student learning."

> From 4.1 – The first three guiding principles "enable teachers to take full advantage of classroom instructional time, for students are then fully engaged, focused, and motivated to learn and achieve."

Paul sat back, soaking in his friend's counsel. It all seemed logical. It made sense that he'd been trapped in a cycle of negativity, and that he could create a new cycle. And it was incredibly appealing to think of not worrying about student behavior and just focusing on learning. And yet while he could clearly visualize the goal, it still seemed so distant. It was a 300 game to a novice bowler. How could he possibly get from the near disaster he'd just had with his eighth graders to that far off fairy land of educational idealism? And yet he believed his friend. Thus far Kris had been right in everything she'd said. If she believed in him, perhaps it wasn't so farfetched. He just needed some practical steps; he needed some concrete ideas he could readily implement so he could begin to see some progress.

"Okay Kris," Paul prepared to level with her, "I see where I need to be, and I also see where I currently am. I need something practical now. We've talked quite a lot of philosophy and metaphoric ideals; give me something concrete that I can implement right away. I'm ready."

Kris nodded in return, sensing the sincerity. "Alright then. The first step on the path to becoming positive is to stop being negative. Sounds simple, but let's be specific. I want you to tell me three student misbehaviors in class today that annoyed you."

"Only three?" joked Paul. "Alright. Tapping pencils, talking to neighbors, and leaving seats without asking."

"Those are perfect," answered Kris. "We're going to take each one and apply them to a three-pronged process of reinforcing the positive. Like a fork, each prong plays an essential role. The first prong is to ignore inconsequential behavior. The second is to recognize desired behavior. The third is to properly address consequential misbehavior. So let's take your examples and apply them to the process, starting with leaving seats without asking. So, what's your class expectation on getting out of seats?"

"That they can't, well, without asking at least."

"What if they need a tissue?"

"I guess I haven't thought it through that detailed. I suppose they should ask, since that's the expectation."

"That's good. You should always hold fast to your expectations. Yet Paul, is it really that big of a deal if an eighth grader quietly gets up, heads to the back of the room for a tissue, and then quickly returns to her seat?"

"I guess if it was quick and quiet, and she didn't distract anyone else."

"So perhaps it's the expectation that is flawed," Kris reasoned. "Or maybe it's not necessarily flawed, it's just not fully clear. The main point, Paul, is that some behavior in the classroom is simply inconsequential. The student is not negatively or positively impacting anyone's success, including their own. And yet sometimes, we as teachers, view such things as defiance and treat them as insubordination. How dare they get a tissue without asking! Don't they know my rules? And then we jump on their case with a glare, a reminder, or even an insult. And in so doing, what's the effect on that student?"

"They feel picked on and perhaps a bit confused."

"Exactly. Their trust for you is diminished and some sand from your walls is pulled to the bottom of your fortress, shrinking their capacity to succeed. Likewise, it impacts the rest of the class. Though they weren't the primary target, they see it and feel the effects."

"And all of that could have been avoided had I just ignored it," concluded Paul.

"Of course this presupposes that you have clearly communicated expectations. And needless to say it also presupposes that the student wasn't goofing off while up getting the tissue; that of course would be defined as consequential misbehavior that would need to be addressed."

"Alright. Good. I see how I could easily get caught up in needless harping. If I'm uptight, I jump on any little thing."

"And when you think through the details, you'll be surprised how much student behavior can simply be ignored." Kris paused to gather her thoughts while Paul tossed in another candy. "Now, you may be wondering about consequential misbehavior. What if that student getting the tissue is goofing around? What about calling out, talking to neighbors, and note passing? How do we address those?"

"I assume you won't be recommending my patented 'yell-until-they're-scared' technique. Right?" Paul quipped.

"You're getting to know me pretty well!" Kris replied, amused. "So yes, no yelling. However, we're going to save the discussion of addressing consequential misbehavior for another time. First, I want you to focus on the first two prongs of reinforcing the positive. The first, of course, being to ignore inconsequential behavior. The second is recognizing desired behavior."

Paul grinned sarcastically, "So being positive doesn't just mean to not be negative?"

"Of course not. It is basic human nature, especially in children, to desire the attention of others. This desire often manifests itself through attention seeking behavior, especially when seeking attention from an admired adult."

"The key word being 'admired.' That's part of that classroom culture thing, right?"

"Certainly. Now let's take another one of your student misbehaviors from yesterday, pencil tapping. Depending on the circumstances, we could argue that this is inconsequential and could be ignored. But instead let's assume that it's really bothering other students and needs to be stopped. What's your natural way to handle this?"

"Easy. Tell him to stop."

Kris shook her head. "That's unfortunately what most teachers do. The problem here is that by so doing you gave him attention. Remember, students want that attention, whether from you or to show off for peers. He got the attention he sought, and he just might do it again to see another rise from you or to get some laughs from his buddies."

"So basically," concluded Paul, "I just reinforced the very behavior that I was trying to stop. But how can I possibly stop it without addressing it?"

"You give attention elsewhere. Openly compliment the student sitting next to your pencil tapper. That compliment should not address his pencil since you'd obviously be indirectly addressing the behavior anyway. But instead offer the neighbor, or the class at large, sincere praise for being on task. Most every time that student, especially if you have a positive relationship, will shape up and stop tapping his pencil."

> From 3.1 – "Teachers ... should reinforce the positive, thereby increasing the likelihood of [desired behavior] being repeated."

"So you stop the misbehavior by ignoring it and complimenting others? Interesting. Does that really work? Even with ego-centric eighth graders?"

"Especially with ego-centric eighth graders! It all depends on your consistency and relationship. However, simply ignoring the one and praising the other doesn't complete the correction. To improve the chances that the misbehavior won't occur in the future, within a matter of seconds after the tapping has stopped, go to that student and whisper sincere, individual praise. 'Thanks, Joe, for your great work today.' 'Great job staying with us, Joe. I appreciate your diligence.' It is incredible how something so simple can prove so meaningful."

"Wow," Paul reflected. "As my old way of just telling him to stop would weaken our relationship and damage his learning while really only stopping the misbehavior temporarily, I can see how this more positive approach would do the opposite. It strengthens relationships and learning while actually eliminating the misbehavior. It seems so simple. How come most teachers don't do this?"

"It takes training and lots of self-discipline. Honestly, it's much more natural to just go put a stop to the misbehavior. We see a problem, we fix it. That's who we are. But now you see there's a better way, and as simple as it sounds right now, I promise you, it's much more challenging to put into practice. You have to be committed and self-aware. You have to constantly self-analyze and self-regulate to develop this new habit. And yet, I can also promise that it is worth it."

"*A new habit. A new culture,*" mused Paul to himself.

> From 3.4.2 – "The warmth of your countenance and kindness of your words strengthens relationships and empowers students to reach high to achieve the expectations."

"And in so doing you'll soon find that it becomes a part of you. You won't just be complimenting students only to correct someone else's misbehavior. You'll be complimenting them with sincerity all the time, even when everyone is behaving well. And trust me, when you're consistent and sincere, they will respond."

Paul sat back unashamedly flashing an entranced smile. What was once a lofty, fairytale goal now seemed completely attainable. He recognized the challenges before him, yet he now felt motivated and equipped with the proper tools to make the change.

Paul's hawk-eyes narrowed in on a small group of girls, quietly snickering in the back of the room. Since their teacher was changing his boundaries, the girls now ventured to test them with this once unthinkable offense. Out of habit, their whisperings beckoned his merciless retaliation. With his claws extended, Paul's instincts told him to strike.

Yet, he hesitated. The voice of his new mentor restrained his punitive impulses. Kris's words rang in his ears and urged him to withdraw his cocked talons.

So, there sat the girls, aware their distracting behavior merited their teacher's attention, yet unaware of the internal struggle they'd elicited. And there stood Mr. Paul Lowry, science teacher, at another personal crossroads. He was caught between the air and the branch, aggression and restraint, habit and change. He knew the road to take, which happened to be the road less traveled, but he stood lost in the indecision of his wavering courage.

"Any sign of Paul today?" Sheri inquired as she nibbled on her celery sticks smeared with peanut butter. "He's usually the first one here for lunch."

"Perhaps working on some lesson plans," replied Alex, looking around the teacher's lounge.

"Yeah, and one of your football players actually qualified for the state math competition." Trisha said sarcastically from a nearby table, again making the most of her opportunity to climb a little higher by pressing others a little lower. "My bet is he's either asleep at his desk or pestering Mr. Phippen to give him a student teacher next semester so he can disappear until retirement."

Journal Entry – October 14

It worked! That crazy counselor's outlandish advice worked! Who could have guessed you can stop bad behavior without ever addressing it? But it worked, and it worked well.

The girls' chatter made me want to knock those bowling pins out with a solid sixteen pounder, but I resisted. And I about fainted from holding my breath, but I resisted. So when I actually trusted myself enough to open my mouth, I smiled, ignored the babbling, complimented the 'vast majority' of the class for paying attention, and continued teaching.

The silence from my hesitation seemed to get the girls' attention, and my compliment to the class seemed to catch them off guard. Perhaps they were at a loss for words at hearing me actually say something nice, but either way, they immediately shaped up. I then worked my way back to their table and thanked them for sticking with the class.

Once I got back to the front, I looked back to see their jaws slopped open in disbelief at my behavior. I wouldn't be surprised if mine had done the same at theirs. They were on task the rest of class. Who would have thought?

> From 3.4.1 – "This process redirects undesired behavior without ever addressing it, and culminates with a relationship strengthening interaction."

Journal Entry – October 28

It's been several weeks now since I've been implementing Kris's ideas of managing behavior by reinforcing the positive. The change for me has been challenging to say the least. I sometimes argue with myself what has been the hardest – ignoring the inconsequential behavior that I'm used to recognizing, or recognizing the desired behavior that I'm used to ignoring. The debate usually ends once the pressure in my head feels as heavy as my bowling ball.

Yet here we are, a week into my self-inflicted migraine sentence, and I'm honestly seeing some real success. Students smile as they enter my room (and I greet them with a smile in return). They participate in lessons and activities (which means I'm actually conducting lessons and activities). They say goodbye to me as they leave (and I do the same for them). As hard as this change has been, it is quite invigorating. I'm sensing a shift in my classes. Where I once reigned with fear, we now interact quite comfortably. And as crazy as it is to admit, I find myself enjoying teaching again – despite the headaches.

> From 2.2.2 – "Kids are kids, and they relate better with those who are friendly."

Now, I know I still have a long way to go to make these first two prongs of reinforcing the positive a habit, but I've come far enough to see the benefits and to be motivated to keep it up. Yet, in making these changes, I see a real need for Kris's third prong, addressing consequential misbehavior. Although my newfound smile has produced some good results, I've also noticed a few negative side effects. The more I remove fear, the more empowered they seem to feel, both for good and for bad. My students sometimes act as if they now have more license to misbehave, which mostly consists of chatting with friends. It's like I've removed the bumpers from the bowling lane; they're having a hard time adjusting to life with less solid boundaries.

There's only so much I can ignore and only so many reminders through compliments I can give. I need an effective, positive way to address their misbehavior to maintain classroom expectations and reaffirm those now somewhat blurred boundaries. Then, I think, the walls of my sand fortress will become more solid.

Paul leaned back in one of the white leather chairs, his feet resting comfortably atop the table separating him from Kris. The ease of conversation between the two now stood in striking contrast to their first few uncomfortable sessions. What was once tense and terse was now normal and natural. Other than Kris's encouraging disposition, the only similarity was the shared KitKat they routinely enjoyed together.

Kris had gained Paul's complete trust and confidence. The positive changes in his classes were a direct result of her counsel. Indeed, Counselor

Kris had become a true confidant and friend. This is why Paul sat still and listened intently to Kris explain her third and final prong of reinforcing the positive. Having reviewed the need for clear and high expectations, Paul sat eager to receive instruction on properly addressing consequential misbehavior.

"Assuming your expectations are high and clearly understood, there will come times, as you've undoubtedly experienced, when students will break your expectations to the point where it needs to be addressed. Ignoring such consequential misbehavior would blur your expectations and weaken your culture."

Paul nodded in agreement. "So," continued Kris, "what sorts of behavior do you think we're talking about here?"

Having seen enough over the years, Paul immediately spouted off a list. "Persistent chatter, blurting out, disrespectful comments, not doing the work, and of course more significant issues like fighting."

"Yes, I'd agree that in most circumstances those couldn't be ignored," replied Kris. "Also, we're not necessarily referring to major infractions that would need more drastic intervention, like an office referral, as those are out of the norm. This approach is for the more common issues that can be handled in class."

> From 3.3 – "It behooves a teacher to identify that which is consequential [and] address them as outlined."

Paul's face broke out into a devious grin. "So are you teaching Mr. Phippen how to handle his job too?"

Kris shook her head. "Well, no. Yet these principles could certainly be applied in the office as well."

"Principles for Principals. Sounds like a best seller to me!"

"Creative," Kris giggled, "for a science teacher, anyway." Feigning insult, Paul playfully tossed a balled up candy wrapper in her direction.

Kris regrouped from the friendly banter. "So, you've got a student that keeps blurting out answers and other needless commentary, breaking your class standards. I'd like to teach you a four step method of addressing that consequential misbehavior. But first, you must learn a few guiding principles."

"More principles? Okay, shoot. Or just tell me them, I mean. Let's leave Mr. Phippen unharmed."

Kris again smiled at Paul's once concealed wit; the more comfortable he grew, the more pleasant he became. "Good idea. So, the first thing to remember when addressing their behavior is the absolute priority to maintain the student's dignity. By this I mean that our disciplinary measures should build and strengthen instead of demean and belittle. Eye rolling, talking down, insulting, and the like have no place in a positive classroom culture, and yet, these teacher retaliations are unfortunately commonplace in many schools. Though these actions may temporarily stop the misbehavior, they damage relationships and diminish the student's dignity."

> From 3.5.1 – "Treat the student as they may become, remembering they only briefly forgot their own expectations and potential."

"Build up instead of tear down. Seems hard to do when they've gotten themselves in trouble."

"Just like the first two prongs of reinforcing the positive, it's only hard if you're out of the habit," Kris reminded. "Now, the second principle is to address the behavior in as private a setting as possible. This limits the peer attention they may be seeking, and it helps maintain their dignity."

Kris took a breath and continued explaining. "And finally, the last principle is to strive to get *them* to do the majority of the talking. It seems to be an adult's nature to want to tell a kid what to do and do all the talking ourselves. We think they must hear us because we hear ourselves. When in reality, they're just enduring the tongue-lashing until it's over, caring more about survival than self-improvement. However, your conversation will have the greatest impact when the students themselves vocalize their infraction, name the standard they broke, and explain how they plan to fix it."

Paul summarized, "Maintain dignity. As private as possible. They talk. Got it. So, am I ready for the method now?"

Kris was impressed by Paul's attentiveness. "In essence, I just told you. Through effective questioning, help them vocalize three things: First, what they did wrong, second, why it was wrong, or the standard they broke, and third, how they plan to fix it. I call it the 'What, Why, How' method."

"Okay, let me walk this through with the case scenario of our blurtatious student."

Kris gave Paul a playful, warning look in response to that potentially demeaning remark.

"Not an insult! Just an identifying description. Dignity maintained, I promise!" After having obtained an approving smile, Paul continued. "So this blurta… uh, student who exhibits the tendency to blurt out, needs a little talking to. I need to do it in private, so I quietly go to him and whisper we need to chat during the next class activity. During that time I invite him to the back of the room where I ask him what the reason is for our discussion. He might need a little prodding, but once he acknowledges his blurtatious tendencies, I ask why his blurtificness would be cause for concern. He rattles off class standards like maintaining attention and raising hands. I then further prod regarding how he plans to curtail any future blurtology, to which he outlines his plan. Does that about sum it up?"

"That does it!" responded Kris, stifling a laugh, "but you'll have to maintain a straight face of course!"

"Hey, I've got about two decades worth of students who've only seen my face straight. I think I'll manage."

"I'm sure you will! Now, there's a number of ways you can have this conversation depending on circumstances. It can be done at the student's desk, after class, before or after school, at a conference with a parent, etc. It all depends on the student, the infraction, and other situational circumstances. Also, don't forget the method's last step. The first three are the questions and the student's response; the last is where you get to talk."

"I talk? Finally!"

"Yes, you get to talk, but be brief! The last step is to express surprise and disappointment for their misbehavior as well as confidence in their plan to fix it."

"And is it safe to assume you'll also tell me to complement their newly controlled blurtatious mouth and recognize other appropriate behavior?"

"You're learning well!" answered Kris with pride.

"You know I only come here for the candy, right?"

"That's why I keep it around!"

Journal Entry – December 21

This afternoon I've been packing up some things to bring home for Christmas break. In so doing, I can't help but think about the more extensive packing I'll need to do this summer. Retirement nears. Well, it looms, really. As it was once a thrilling idea, the thought of it now confuses me. I'm no longer certain that's really what I want.

Though I definitely look forward to doing new things with the extra time, my main drive to retire was to get away from the stresses of teaching. For me, it was more about running away than running to.

Yet now, here I am, not long into this classroom culture shift. These new strategies that are just beginning to take hold have not only made positive changes for my students, they are changing me as well. Yep, that grumpy old science instructor is just now learning the joys of real teaching.

And yet I'm just beginning; I'm just now learning. I'm just starting to really teach and enjoy my students' success. I feel as if I'm fresh out of college, and this is my first year all over again. How can I

> From 3.4.2 – "With each sincere compliment, recognition, and word of praise, your habits will change and your culture of success will strengthen."

leave after I've just begun? How can I walk away when I'm just now figuring out what I wish I'd known decades ago? Why would I run away when the thing I'm running away from is really where I want to be?

I'll need time to think through these questions during the break. Perhaps I'll have to withdraw from the Holly Jolly Bowling Tournament!

The halls of East Crossroads were filled to capacity. Students hurried about locating the friends they'd missed during Christmas break. Dressed in new clothes and flashing new trinkets, the swelling flock of teenage humanity eagerly showed off their new loot like, well, like eager teenagers after Christmas break. Upon entering the school, they had all instantly shed any ill effects of their altered sleeping schedules from the break, and filled the halls with electric, uncontrolled energy in the way that only young teenagers can.

In a corner near the entrance to the library, a small group of girls contributed to the scene with their own version of boundless energy. Squeals, screams, and squeezes hallmarked the reunion from the painful fourteen day absence. Now reunited, Kim and her two best friends eventually calmed down enough to revel in the thought that their eighth grade year was now half over. Swerving from one topic to the next, the general theme of their conversation included the end of middle school, the prospects of summer, and the excitement of high school to follow. Homework, boys, tests, teachers, all were merely inconvenient potholes on their drive to the future.

However, Kim reserved her opinion that some of those potholes weren't potholes at all. Boys? Well, sure. Nothing good about those slovenly creatures. But her teachers? There were some who were so influential that she wondered how she could ever go on without them.

One, in particular, she had grown to admire with great sincerity. This teacher had motivated her in ways she had not previously experienced. He was caring, kind, witty, engaging, and absolutely dedicated to her success.

The crazy thing was, the man had the reputation similar to that of *The Grinch Who Stole Christmas.* Mr. Lowry had been made out to be mean, demeaning, and more concerned about making his students fear him than actually teaching. And quite honestly, Kim had to admit that he lived up to that reputation for the first couple months. The only thing that stood out more than his menacing eyes had been the various editions of his stupid bowling magazines. Indeed, Mr. Lowry had been the Grinch, the Grinch who stole their education.

Why or how he began to change, Kim didn't know. Yet gradually she had observed a shift in her science teacher's behavior. At first he began to come out from behind his desk a little more (which made her scared of some ulterior motive). Then he tried an experiment or two (an obvious concern to her unsinged hair and overall health and appearance). He eventually started smiling (showing his unexpectedly normal-sized K-9 teeth), and the transformation continued from there.

Over the course of several weeks, Mr. Lowry had somehow transformed himself from Grinch to Great. Students saw much less of their textbooks and much more of their lab books. They sat much less at their tables and stood much more at their experiment stations. They saw much less of his bowling magazines and much more of his lighter side.

It had taken Kim and her classmates a while to trust the shift in their once tyrant of a teacher. But over time, his consistency showed them that his new self was for real. And in so doing, they had reciprocated with renewed positive behavior of their own. Kim noticed how her classmates, many of whom regularly acted up in other classes, were consistently on task for Mr. Lowry. They listened, participated, learned, and behaved. The more pleasant their teacher became, the better her classmates seemed to respond. Science was becoming fun again.

When the warning bell rang, Kim and her two friends reluctantly parted ways to head to first period. Their paths crossed regularly throughout the day, producing more squeals of delight. And yet silently Kim was most

> From 2.2.2 – A friendly teacher "is warm, welcoming, happy, and approachable."

delighted at the thought of seventh period science after the two week absence. She was excited to see her teacher again. She was excited to see what experiments and discoveries their new semester would bring.

The day pushed onward, as days tended to do, until the bell finally announced the beginning of seventh period. Kim and her classmates hurried to their seats, retrieved their lab books, and waited eagerly for their teacher to begin.

Mr. Lowry had been talking in the back with some sixth period students who needed a little assistance wrapping up their activity. After some playful high fives, the group scurried out of the room sporting smiles to go with their new clothes.

Mr. Lowry took his place at the front of the class. Before beginning, he scanned the room with the look of a proud and loving grandfather. To Kim, the look said it all. She was in for another semester of an exhilarating science class.

And to Paul, the attentive and eager appearance of his students also said it all. The decision he had made over the break, was now confirmed.

Chapter Four Author's Note

Okay, so Paul is a little extreme. However, take a moment and think of your own education. Did you ever have a teacher like him? Is there anyone like that in your current school? What about you? Do you have a little negativity to be rid of? Though there are relatively few teachers as extreme as Mr. Lowry, most can see at least a small piece of him in themselves.

This being true, where do you begin? Chances are you don't need a drastic transformation like Paul. So start with an honest look inward and identify the small areas of needed growth. Then, look to this universal principle of reinforcing the positive, seek to understand its intent and applications, and commit to, at minimum, making an effort. The full implementation of the principle takes time. Consciously and purposefully make the effort until, with time, it becomes a habit. Our class culture will shift parallel with our own.

Now, does reinforcing the positive contradict the principle of intrinsic motivation? Isn't verbal praise just another extrinsic motivator? Perhaps, if used incorrectly. In chapter three, Alex Clemmington learned that the goal of intrinsic motivation is to separate students from dependence on temporary external bribes and instead build lasting internal self-motivation. When a teacher reinforces the positive correctly, they point the finger of success back at the student. They bring to students' understanding the benefits of their efforts and the direct relationship between their work and their success. Reinforcing the positive does not build up the teacher, it builds up the student. It stirs within them their own self-worth, strengthening their inner-drive to succeed. Thus, as with all the guiding principles, they are not to be considered as separate entities, but an inter-woven fabric of unified compliments.

Our students not only need our love and devotion, they need to hear and feel it from us every day. We can create welcoming, nurturing environments where students from all backgrounds can feel welcome and appreciated. Will they still goof around? Probably. Will they fail to do their best?

At times. But our efforts to build students' self-image and confidence will have more long lasting, positive effects than any dangling carrot could possibly accomplish.

Indeed, our task is monumental, but that is the challenge we accept when we set foot in a classroom. Millions of parents send us their children, who are with us longer each day than they are with their parents. They, therefore, trust us to help ensure the growth and success of their children. The public trust sits in desks inside our classrooms, and we can most certainly bowl a strike.

Questions to Consider – Your Journal Entry #3

1. How do students feel when they enter my classroom? Do my interactions with them tend to be more positive or negative? Do they know I like them and have confidence in them? How?

2. What student behavior bugs me? What behavior is inconsequential that can be ignored and what is consequential that I should address? When addressing misbehavior, how can I do so in a manner consistent with the principle of reinforcing the positive?

3. How often do I recognize appropriate student behavior? Has doing so, both verbally and otherwise, become a habit? What will I do to increase my positive student interactions?

Chapter Five

Trisha and the Principle of Student-Centered Instruction

> **Student-Centered Instruction** – Instructional methods focus on the needs of individual students for the ultimate goal of individual student success.

Vanity. There it stands, smooth and refined where visible yet jagged and tactless everywhere else. It steps on friends to find a stage and still envies anyone at the podium. It seeks out the flattery of those in lead roles, likewise of those backstage. It inflates each compliment to a standing ovation. Each word of advice or friendly feedback either cuts deep, builds a grudge, or is fully denied. Vanity. It is the quagmire of judgment. It is the vapor that clouds one's reality. And though many are able to thin the mists, there are those who, quite unknowingly, wallow in its shadowy influence.

Enter stage left – Dr. Trisha LaValle. She had spent her days on the stage of life taking well deserved bows. Her lists of accomplishments stretched from elementary spelling bee champion to high school valedictorian to PhD magna cum laude. With every honor, she soaked up the accompanying applause like a bloated sponge.

And as the years progressed and the honors mounted, to her the sweet taste of peer recognition had become more important than the personal satisfaction of a job well done. It was as if the words – and envy – of others fueled her drive to become the main attraction. And yet she was blind to the irony of seeking praise from the unpraiseworthy, from those she deemed beneath her.

Yes, she was Dr. Trisha LaValle, bright and bold. She insisted on being called by her full name, Trish-a; for if you cut off the "a," you cut off her identity.

Trisha sat near the back corner of the teachers' lounge, calmly correcting a pile of math homework while sipping her lightly sweetened bottled water. She was keenly aware of several pointed looks and whispers, though she most certainly pretended she wasn't. It was rare for her to eat lunch with her colleagues in the lounge. She found it easier to maintain her well-manicured reputation if she refrained from common chit chat with the support cast.

The first week of school was coming to a close. It had been similar to all the others she'd experienced during her ten years at East Crossroads. Her colleagues fluttered about in an effort to survive the immense challenges of the beginning days of school. The ill effects of their lazy summer vacations combined with the barrage of unruly students produced a teachers' lounge suffering from the odd mixture of scrambling to keep up and resting to wind down. All felt the need for both, but none seemed able to do either effectively.

These conclusions were the product of Trisha's vain musings. She enjoyed sitting back and observing the anxiety, and she enjoyed even more witnessing that anxiety increase as other teachers perceived her own calm. She was fine, and they knew that she was.

Trisha's uptight demeanor was exemplified by her pointed, upturned nose coupled with her pitch-black hair pulled back in a tight bun; for yes, her nose was up and her bun was tight. The persona was further defined by her interchangeable suit ensembles that exuded professionalism with a hint of royalty. Yet unlike most queens, Trisha wore her crown on her feet. Her wardrobe's most prized element were her bold-colored, high heeled shoes that clicked in harmony to announce her approach. She loved the attention brought on by her heels and reputation, well, she loved the attention from all but one.

"Well now, welcome to the teachers' lounge Little Miss Trish!" blurted Paul, purposefully shortening her name to enjoy the irked look that regularly followed. "How kind of you to grace us with your presence. What, did you come to rummage through the supplies to find polish for your Teacher of the Year plaque? You know, toilet cleaner could do the trick too. The janitor's closet is just around the corner."

Trisha first responded with a look of feigned amusement. The persistent banter between the two had become routine over the years. And though playful in nature, both knew there was some truth to the teasing.

"No need, thank you," she replied. "I still have plenty of polish left over from what came with my first plaque. And come to think of it, I've got even more from the two I've earned since. I'd be happy to lend you some for your bowling trophies, but from what I gather you're as bad in the bowling alley as you are in your science lab, so your trophy case must be empty. But hey, I'd be happy to pick up a dust rag for you!"

The few awkward snickers at Trisha's zinger sounded much louder in her ears than what they were in reality.

—∞—

"Welcome to East Crossroads you two!" Kris exclaimed from the comfort of her white, leather chair. "Here's a copy of your schedules and a school map. Seth, you'll see that the bulk of your eighth grade classes are along the north wing. Sarah, you'll primarily be on the south end in the sixth grade hall. Seth, can I trust you'll help your sister find her way?"

Seth dropped his head, letting his shaggy, dirty blond hair fall past his eyes as if to veil himself to the world. His disconsolate expression combined with his ripped jeans and skater hoodie boldly proclaiming "Scars are Just Cheap Tattoos," completed his forced front of teenage independence. Though his mouth never moved, Counselor Kris could almost hear the boy say, "Back off. This is my life."

Additionally, Seth's records revealed that he and his sister had been to five different schools in the last four years. Such transitions were never easy, especially a couple of weeks into the year. And Kris could tell that any semblance of excitement for change had long since been snuffed out. Here sat a kid, outwardly wearing his inner frustrations like a rusted over 1970-something diesel. Dirty. Lonely. Broken.

Having received no answer to her question, Kris responded to the silence. "Yet, it looks like you two might see each other around fourth period when you both have math. Mr. Harding and Dr. LaValle have classrooms right across the hall from each other. That should be nice to see a friendly face each day while you two get settled in."

Seth responded with a small nod that was exaggerated by his disheveled hair. Subtly turning from the stubborn mop to his sister, Kris offered Sarah a considerate smile. Clearly unsurprised by her brother's desultory demeanor, Sarah glanced between him and the school counselor with a look of dejection. She eventually feigned a half smile in return, grabbed both their schedules, and trailed her brother out of the office.

Kris followed to the point of her open office doorway. Watching the two file out to the reception area of the Counselor Corner and then to the empty halls of the school they'd been forced to brave, she could barely overhear their hushed conversation.

"She was nice, Seth. Why didn't you say anything?"

Silence.

"Why not at least give this school a try? You haven't flunked anything here; you've got a fresh start."

Silence.

"Seth, come on. School's not all that bad if you just try."

Silence.

"And hey, you made it into advanced math again. I heard your teacher is real good, hard, but good. We can study together if you'd like."

After another period of silence, a low rumble eventually muttered, "Last time I actually try on a placement test."

A stream of students flowed into the classroom, each grabbing a half sheet warm up exercise from a tray sitting atop a neatly organized table just inside the door. Hurrying to their assigned seats placed perfectly square in neat rows facing the front white board, the students threw their books beneath their seats, grabbed a pencil, and began vigorously working on their warm ups. They could see the timer was already counting down, moving, it seemed, more quickly than it was in reality.

But that was the way of eighth grade geometry with the great Dr. LaValle. To her students, her class was like training for the Olympics: push-ups, pull-ups, running, sweating, no walking, no resting, no slowing, no stopping. You sprint to class, hurry to your seat, get right to work, and don't stop until told. No one spoke out of turn, asked too many questions, or told another what they did that weekend. These things just didn't happen with Dr. LaValle. No one challenged it; no one questioned it. It was just the way it was.

And because no one questioned such Olympian standards, the students didn't really seem to mind. There was no time to complain or be off task. To them, the challenge was invigorating, like the rush one might feel from competing in the luge; it was as intense during the moment as it was satisfying once it was over.

> From 1.3.1 – "High academic practices reinforce high behavioral expectations."

There was no ready or set – just go.

Trisha paced up and down the rows, keeping a close eye on her students' progress. With less than two minutes remaining, she felt a twinge of frustration at their runner-up pace. She expected more. Yet, she calmly suppressed it, telling herself it was just the first week of school. She still had 176 more days with these students, enough time to whip them into shape. End of year testing was on her mind, even in August. There wasn't a moment to lose if she was going to again score first in the district.

The timer sounded. With a rush, each student dropped their pencil and grabbed a red pen. Without a word, one student reset the timer, while another placed an answer sheet on the screen that was projected for all to see. With their teacher still calmly circling about, the students frantically reviewed their work and wrote their score at the top.

Upon another beep of the timer, each student handed their papers to the back of the rows. One student collected them and placed the stack back in the tray where they had originated. Each student then opened their textbook, retrieved some note paper, and sat awaiting the day's lesson, thankful for a chance to catch their breath.

"Seven minutes. Not bad."

While a casual observer might be relatively impressed by the pace, a trained eye would marvel at this classroom machine. The details of the interworking parts combined together for a cohesive system with a singular purpose – speed. Each procedure had been orchestrated and implemented to maximize each available moment. And at this point in the class, Dr. LaValle seemingly hadn't done a thing. She didn't have to. She had taken the time earlier in the week to establish exactly what she expected, and now all that was needed was some fine tuning to shave off a few seconds each day.

"Next week, I expect it to take no more than five."

Dr. LaValle's three-inch heels clacked their way to the front of the class where she assumed her position at the left side of the white board, ready to sprint through the day's lesson. The students braced themselves for the race ahead. They knew the board would be filled several times over before they'd find reprieve at the finish line of the dismissal bell.

As usual, she reached for the purple marker, signifying the royalty that she felt she was. Black was the only other color she occasionally uncorked, mostly as an undertoned signal to step it up. The purple was her, so she used it most. The black was everyone else, so she used it least, and only as a source of warning that the purple wasn't pleased.

"Today we learn about complementary and supplementary angles. Here's our first example. Suppose $m<A = 43^0$. How much bigger is the supplement of $<A$ than the complement? Okay, let's get right to it…"

The students feverishly worked to keep up with the herculean pace. Barely defining the critical terms themselves, Dr. LaValle blazed from example to example with the subconscious supposition that all was understood. Angles, segments, bisectors, they were all presented in majestic purple. She felt it her duty to present the material and her students' duty to understand it. And therefore, the more material she presented, the more they'd have the opportunity to understand.

And therein lied the problem.

"Dr. LaValle," softly queried a boy with his hand in the air. His teacher turned her head in the direction of the interruption, her hand still firmly pressing the purple marker against the board's quickly diminishing white space. Her pointed nose conducted the brief search. Upon locating the boy, she forced a grin and nodded her head, her hand still pressed against the board.

"I'm still struggling with the difference between the terms complementary and supplementary. Can you go back and explain, just for a sec?" Many other students nodded in agreement, happy they weren't the ones to voice the request.

> From 4.2.2 – A self-centered teacher does "not consider the unique needs of their class... Their lesson delivery is methodical and inflexible."

The doctor looked around the room. Her arm sagged against the board. Go back? Really? A hurdle was one thing; it may slow you down a bit, but you can still just jump over it. But going back? During a race? Unheard of.

With a small roll of the eyes and lift of the nose, Dr. LaValle recapped her royal wand and turned in the direction of her students. She inhaled deeply and clacked her heels back to the other side of the board.

Pointing her capped imperial baton at the pertinent information, she explained in veiled irritation, "Like I said before, complementary angles are two angles that add up to 90 degrees. Supplementary angles add up to 180." Then, resisting the urge to leave it at that, she continued, "An easy way to remember is that C comes before S, just like 90 comes before 180."

The collective "oh" from the class stroked her ego a bit, but it didn't completely curb her annoyance. To Trisha, the students' reaction was a cross between a gasp for the champion's slowed pace and applause for the mercy she'd showed her lagging competitors. With renewed energy, she clacked her way back to where she'd left off. Now with the bun of her hair slightly disheveled, she unleashed the black marker, pressed it against the remaining white space, and sprinted to the finish line.

"Four students! That's four incomplete homework assignments!"

The students buckled under the unusual outburst from their geometry teacher. They were caught by surprise because this wasn't the Dr. LaValle they'd known for the first two weeks. She had always been challenging and tough, not rude and angry. The students had enjoyed the exhilarating pace, as challenging as it was. That's what they had signed up for. But this? Their shock was as intense as Dr. LaValle's bold red heels, which at the moment oddly mirrored the fire in her eyes.

> From 1.2.2 – "Do not [review expectations] as a reaction to a breach; instead, do so in a positive manner, complimenting students on living up to the expectations."

"There are twenty-two students in this class. Do you know what percentage that is? Almost 20%! Nearly one fifth of you! That's not my standard. You were placed in my class, my accelerated class, because you identified yourselves as those who could keep up. I will not allow my classes to become mediocre. I expect 100% homework completion every day of every week for the entire year! Are we clear?"

The few seconds of silence that followed were elongated by the aggravated tapping of Dr. LaValle's heel, but eventually and collectively, the students began to nod their heads in submission.

"So, yes?" inquired Dr. LaValle, striving to calm herself. "100% homework? Do I have your word?"

The students again responded with more nods and a smattering of repentant "yes's." Today they'd seen a new side of Dr. LaValle, and they didn't want to see it again. The queen could crack, and when she did, her subjects paid the penalty. Completing homework was a small price to pay to avoid such royal outrage.

—∞—

That afternoon Trisha burst into the teachers' lounge, nearly knocking over Mr. Phippen as she dashed to the fridge in a huff, trying to ignore the startled eyes staring at her from all sides of the room.

> From 1.3.2 – "In reality, a student who forgets their homework a single time isn't necessarily choosing a life path of failure."

Paul jumped on the obvious instability of his nemesis, smelling an easy victory. "Well, well, little Trishy. You've got to be careful who you push aside. Isn't your tactic to schmooze the higher-ups while stepping on the rest of us peons?"

Trisha was clearly unable to control her fragile temperament after the uncharacteristic lashing she'd dished out last period. To Trisha, the only thing worse than losing control was having others notice. Her reputation was everything, and now she was on the edge of damaging it. And as hard as it was to keep her mouth closed at Paul's aggression, a retaliation would certainly further reveal her fragile emotions. No. She'd just retrieve her lunch, retreat to her throne room, and sulk until she could find her way home and let her sleep do the dirty work of calming her down.

—∞—

As always, the students rushed to their seats and began their warm up, propelled to perform by the rigorous standards to which they'd become accustomed over the first few weeks of school. Complete the warm up, turn in homework, take notes on the day's new lesson — and do it all at warp speed.

Trisha had managed to regain her footing after last week's stumble. Her students had responded with resilience, and she'd managed to escape revealing weakness to her colleagues. All was back to normal, and they were back to enjoying the admiration of the school at large.

Now, when beginning training, the Olympic sprinter is daily pushed to the point of exhaustion. With each strenuous workout, his muscles burn and his lungs gasp for mercy. Yet with persistent, steady training, over time his strength and stamina allow him to turn what was once quite impossible into a mere warm up.

> From 2.2.1 – "Students generally perform to the measure of their immediate environment, whether high or low."

Such was the case in Dr. LaValle's classes. The consistency of the standards and routines had first challenged even the best of students to the point of discouragement, but now, with time, they had become conditioned to it. Their heart rates slowed and their pain tolerance grew. After weeks of Olympic-style training, the students always finished the warm up in under five minutes, completed their homework, and remained fully attentive. It had all become habit. Sure, they didn't fully understand every concept — they didn't have time to — but they sure could move fast, and fast was fun.

Seconds before the ring of the warm up timer in fourth period geometry, the students were startled by the creaking of the classroom door. As a reflex, Dr. LaValle and her students turned to see the cause of the unpleasant disruption. There stood a young, teenage boy, class schedule in hand, obviously a new addition to this group of budding Olympians.

Dr. LaValle took a step toward the intruder, the echo of her heel snapping the students back to their work. Knowing the routines, the students took care of themselves for the next few minutes as the doctor took care of business.

Sizing him up, Trisha did not like what she saw. Her mind's eye perceived nothing but a lazy lump of wasted teenage space. Floppy, untied skater shoes. Holey, baggy jeans. A dirty hoodie proclaiming in jagged black lettering, "Skaters Only: Violators Will Be KICKFLIPPED!" His ragged, long blond hair eerily protruded from underneath his hood, covering much of his face and concealing what were sure to be apathetic eyes.

To Trisha, his whole persona screamed disruption. Her students had finally conditioned themselves to perform at her standard. They had momentum on their side. But now, this. If this lump were to join their class, he was sure to slow them down. He was a road block, strategically placed to impede their – no, her – success!

Who had done this? Paul? Mr. Phippen? That new school counselor? Surely it must have been some jealous nobody out for blood. She taught geometry… to the eighth graders! That was one of the reasons she demanded all the advanced classes each year. First, how could one of her caliber mingle amongst the peasants of the kingdom? But also, everyone knew how rare it was for new students to qualify for placement in distinguished classes like her own. And if for some miracle they did qualify, they'd have to be geniuses. But now, just look at him. An old stump square in the middle of her imperial gardens. This was a mistake that would soon be rectified. He had to go.

Snatching the schedule from his hand, Dr. LaValle hissed, "Hello. New to school, are you?" Her upturned nose was as pointed as a dagger.

His only response was a shrug and a grunt.

"Well, it appears so. This is advanced placement mathematics, geometry to be precise. These students are all on the course of acceleration: early graduation, full-ride scholarships, collegiate prestige. That's our identity, who we are. Do you feel able to join such an elite group?"

The boy looked up and peered through his ratty hair, seeing only reproach. He held her glare with confident defiance, holding on longer than any previous peasant to its queen. Then eventually, he broke the stare

> From 1.3.2 – "A student breaches expectations when *consistently* breaching standards or procedures or doing so a singular time in a *significant* way."

down with a rebellious swoop of the hair and lumbered his way to the back of the class where he dropped his backpack to the floor with a slam and his head on the desk with a thud.

Dr. LaValle, still perched in place, couldn't have received a clearer answer to her question had he screamed "no" in her face. She turned her nose from the direction of the dormant lump to that of his schedule, still firm in hand. After confirming, yet again, that he'd indeed been placed in her class, her nose made its way to the top of the crinkled paper to identify if this thing now thrust in her way had a name, some sort of identifier she could throw back at the office to be immediately changed or immediately chained – at the moment, either was fine with her.

In clear black letters, the schedule identified the object of her disdain – Seth Gittens.

—m—

Kris sat quietly at her desk, reviewing the beginning of year assessment data from the Language Arts department. Her office door was open to the reception area of the Counselor Corner, the open door functioning as a sign of welcome to those who may desire to enter, student or staff.

Kris was now a few weeks into her first year as a school counselor and her first year at East Crossroads. After several years as a successful classroom teacher, she was now pursuing a new challenge, a new way to be a positive influence on the lives of students. She had hoped that her new role would provide more opportunities to work one on one with students, especially those with greater needs. Her plan had been to jump right in, identifying those with academic or behavioral challenges and be an active support, seeing them through to success.

Yet now, quite unintentionally, she had found herself spending much of her time diverted from students. It had been the teachers of East Crossroads who seemed to be in most need of her services. It had begun with Ms. Sheri Price, with a bang of course, and then Sheri's contagious enthusiasm advertised Kris's worth to the rest. One by one, teachers began to seek her out; not all, but many. And as they kept seeking, she kept receiving. The more she received, the more word seemed to spread. And though she desired a little more time for students, she was enjoying this impromptu role of instructional specialist. However unintentional it had begun, Kris was taking great pleasure in this indirect role of helping students, for helping students was her primary goal.

"Seth Gittens."

Kris looked up to see the face of the most renowned teacher in the school, her contemptuous nose pointing in accusation. Kris had heard the stories and seen the honors posted in the front office. She had also noticed numerous hallway conversations about this woman, conversations of both students and staff. Everyone seemed to know her, and everyone seemed to hold her in high regard. And although they had yet to have much interaction, Kris felt she knew more about Trisha than about anyone else in the school.

"Well, hello there, Dr. LaValle! Trisha, right? I'm thrilled to welcome you to my office. What can I help you with today?"

Trisha flung a crinkled paper on Kris's desk. "Help me? Well, I've actually come to help you. Being new to East Crossroads, you need to better understand how things work in the math department. Mr. Harding and Mrs. Danielson teach the low and mid math classes, the usual place for new move-ins. I teach the advanced classes. Our accelerated groups don't have time for disruptions. Move-ins can't keep up. They don't belong."

> From 4.2.2 – A self-centered teacher "may be selfish with curricula, schedules, and other school-related functions."

Having heard out Trisha's "help," Kris flashed a patient smile and picked up the paper. Upon seeing the name at the top of the student schedule, everything immediately clicked. Seth Gittens. Yes, she had thought this boy would be a challenge. Absent of a single word, he had made it perfectly clear that to him school was torment, forced severance from the real priorities of the life of a teenage skater. This boy needed help. He needed guidance and direction. With Seth, they had a grand opportunity to make a positive impact on his quickly deflating potential.

"Oh yes, Seth Gittens," responded Kris, her pleasant voice rung in stark contrast to Trisha's haughty tone. "We certainly had a stiff initial meeting. It was pretty obvious he wasn't too excited to be here. Yet, that was why I was so thrilled he had tested into your geometry class. He certainly puts on an absent-minded front, but there he is, qualifying for tenth grade math in middle school! How wonderful!"

Trisha's eyes stared down the narrow barrel separating the two. *Wonderful? Was she crazy?* "Look. He may have gotten lucky on the placement test, but that in no way means he is actually qualified to be in my class. He's lost; he's slowing us down. He needs something else, anything else." She resisted the urge to add, "Anywhere else."

Kris cheerily stood her ground. "I can certainly see how he'll have a tough time with the transition. Honestly, wouldn't we all? Moving in mid-year is challenging enough, but to be placed in a class as highly regarded as your own, that will certainly challenge him even more. Yet the assessment truly shows his correct placement. So, with this challenge also comes a great opportunity, an opportunity for both him and you. Trisha, I'm sure a revered teacher like you will do a masterful job. Seth couldn't be in a better situation."

Her vanity took keen note of the compliments, yet still she pressed on for the sake of the big picture. "Better situation? How about a situation

> From 4.3 – "It is… the duty of the student-centered teacher to assess the overall needs of the class, tailor the general instruction to them, and then work to accommodate the needs of the outliers."

"Well then, give him a chance," Kris reasoned. "I've heard of your high standards and quick pacing; that's great! Don't slow down for the rest of your students. Yet also, I'm certain someone who has had as much success as you over the years will do a wonderful job accommodating his unique needs along the way. I'd offer some suggestions, but no doubt you've got plenty of methods you've used over the years. I'm excited for Seth. That boy needs someone with your experience and abilities. He's going to do great."

The flattery struck again, this time with a little more force. Now slightly glowing, Trisha stepped back, looked aside, and aimed her pistol elsewhere. Her frustration lessened as her ego was stroked, and yet she was still unable to fully concede. "Very well. I guess I'll need to review this with the office. Mr. Phippen is better acquainted with the way things work around here."

"That sounds like a good idea. When I reviewed it with Mr. Phippen yesterday, he seemed pretty supportive of the placement. But you're the expert. I'm sure he'll be all ears. Yet honestly Trisha, I hope you get to keep Seth. I'm sure you'll do wonders for him."

Her bun suddenly unable to hide the expansion of her head, Trisha waved her white flag in surrender. She was much more accustomed to the routine cynical banter with Paul; she had trained herself to always be prepared for a rebuttal. This, however, caught her off guard. How do you retaliate against kindness?

Suddenly unsure of herself, Trisha pasted on a half-smile, turned on her heel, and stepped her way out the door. Upon entering the hallway, she stopped and gazed in the direction of the front office. Her pompous self didn't want to give up the fight. Yet, this experience had somehow created within her a foreign sense of indecision. Where before she would already be in Mr. Phippen's office barking curt orders, instead she stood frozen. The path in front of her was the battle; behind her was retreat. In front of her was arrogance; behind her was submission. In front was vanity; behind was change.

—∞—

"Hey Seth, eat this!"

Rounding the corner to East Crossroads, Seth's little sister, Sarah, playfully took off on her bike toward the school, leaving him and his skateboard to slowly bring up the rear. By the time Seth made it to the bike rack, Sarah was sitting on the ground, leaning up against the side of the school using her backpack as a pillow, feigning sleep from the long wait.

Seth grinned at the good-natured display of his cheerful sister. She had always had that impish quality of a carefree child, which was about the only thing in the world that could warm his heart. He looked down at his little sister, smiling through her fake snore, unable to hide the dimple in her right cheek that always appeared at even the slightest presence of a smile. Sarah. To him, she was more his child than his sister. Within him swelled the paternal instincts of support and protection.

With a flick of his foot, Seth kicked up his board and leaned it against the school next to Sarah. He reached into his backpack and pulled out a chain and lock, then tossed the backpack right on his sleeping sister's lap.

"Hey!" she yelped, jumping to her feet. Seth just smiled in return, pleased to hear the sing-song sound of her voice. "Didn't you know it's unsafe to wake someone in the middle of a dream?"

"It's when they're sleepwalking, Einstein."

"Oh yeah, right." Sarah made her way over to the rack where Seth was just about finished locking up her bike. "Wow. I feel refreshed. There's nothing like a nice, long nap before school, wouldn't you say? Oh yeah, you wouldn't know. That skateboard is as slow as Grandma's driving."

Seth responded with a playful push, enjoying his sister's budding wit.

"Seth, really now, we need to get you a bike. Two big wheels are always better than four little ones."

Seth turned to face his sister, peering through his ragged hair. He resisted retaliating with a second push and instead just pointed to his shirt which read, "To Skate or Not To Skate? There Is No Question." To which she responded with a playful push of her own, her twig arms barely able to move the strong torso of her well-worked brother. At that, they both erupted in laughter.

As the climax of their banter settled into normalcy, Seth walked back to the spot of Sarah's pseudo slumber, bent down, and picked up her "pillow." After handing it over, he lifted his own backpack along with his skateboard, and together they made their way to the back entrance of East Crossroads. As they rounded the corner, Sarah offered a question to which she hoped for a response other than the one she expected.

"So, how's your first week of school been?"

Seth's face darkened. He instinctively lowered his head so his hair could cover his eyes and their instant clouding of frustrated anger. How was his first week of school? Really? He hated it. It was just like all the other schools, stupid and useless. All the lessons and lectures were an absolute waste of time. And his teachers! What did they want him to do? Their classes were so boring he couldn't help but fall asleep, but then every time he did they'd come around and wake him up. Talk about hypocrisy!

But worst of all was math. He'd kicked himself all week for actually trying on that idiotic placement test. Despite the string of D's, he knew he was good at math. So when that counselor gave him the test, without realizing the consequences, he didn't blow it off. And his reward for doing well? Geometry...

> From 4.2.2 – A self-centered teacher does "not accommodate individual needs."

Dr. LaValle... death! Ah! That woman needed an ollie to the mouth! She expected him to be some sort of robo-student, shooting out answers like a machine-gun. Screw that. Why should he listen to her incessant nagging? The more she pushed, the more he pushed back. He could tell that their battle would soon come to a head, and there was no way on earth he was going to back down. *Bring it on Doc*, Seth thought to himself. *You don't know me yet.*

As they approached the back entrance to the school in silence, Sarah concluded she didn't need an answer; Seth's clenched fists said it all.

—m—

Trisha glared past the rows of innocent bystanders who, as always, worked diligently on their warm up, back toward the heap of human waste slumped over in his desk at the back of the room. Not only did he not belong, he was slowly sucking the momentum from this once promising group of academics. With each passing day, she was forced to wage battle. He came tardy, ignored instructions, slept through notes, and never completed homework. No matter the amount of coaxing or yelling, his response was either defiant silence or raging argument. Never had a student challenged her standards so. After all, she was Dr. Trisha LaValle, scholar and professor. The endless stream of awards and recognition hadn't come to her by chance. She was the empress of her court, and no previous peasant had ever dared challenge her dominion.

So, what was the queen to do? Seek help? Bah! Reaching out to that gangling jester Mr. Phippen was beneath her dignity. Plus, if word got out of her plight and pathetic call for help, what would happen to her carefully crafted reputation? She knew that it takes years to build a reputation and only seconds to tear it down. No. Her public status was more important than this battle, so however loud it got within her class, she'd keep it quiet without.

Trisha followed her nose to the back of the room, her clacking heels announcing the cavalry's advance. The surrounding students did their best to focus on their task while Seth remained in his usual slumped position. The only visible part of his body was the hair poking out from underneath his hoodie.

Trisha nudged him on the shoulder, "Seth."

Silence.

She did so again, this time with a little more force, "Seth, get up."

Again, silence.

Losing some restraint, Trisha pulled back Seth's hood which revealed his scraggly mane. Slowly, she pushed upwards on his shoulders, lifting him upright. "Seth, get out your homework and notes. It's time for the lesson."

Amazingly, Seth opened his eyes to meet his nemesis. He hadn't done his homework, as always. And he didn't care about the

> From 1.3.2 – "It is a big deal when expectations are breached. Wise and immediate intervention is needed, such as behavior trackers, parent meetings, or office intervention, to name a few."

lesson, as always. He knew he wasn't going to give in to that lurch, so he silently calculated what would be the best battle tactic this time. Passive or aggressive? He'd already had a few shouting matches this week, which were getting a bit old. Plus, he had to save a few of his best insults for later; you know, spread them out a bit. So yeah, passive. He'd go with that one today.

With a role of his eyes, Seth methodically reached down and grabbed his spiral notebook, completely blank. This accomplished his first feat, get the witch out of his grill. Next? He laid his head back down, but this time he turned to the side where he could look at his notebook and fake participation. And as Her Highness began flashing her purple scepter, Seth lazily doodled. Before long, he was halfway through drawing in graffiti-style lettering "sk8 dont hate," when he dropped his pencil and faded back to sleep. The next time his teacher nudged him, he ignored it. Eventually, the bell announced the end of this round of battle, and thus another victory for the rebel skater.

It was lunch time, and Kris was in need of some supplies. She usually avoided the teachers' lounge during lunch, preferring to maintain a professional distance from her colleagues. But at that moment she found herself heading in that direction to retrieve what she needed from the lounge's cupboards, despite her more reclusive nature.

Kris entered and immediately noticed all eyes fall on her. She saw several straighten up and sensed the tone of conversations shift. It was quite clear that word of her influence continued to spread. That had never really been her intention, as she just desired to be of service where needed, but a certain part of her was pleased. She was pleased to be involved in helping teachers better help their students.

There sat Mr. Clemmington. He was really starting to learn that being a mentor was much better than being popular. And Ms. Price, boy, nothing could hold down her enthusiasm. Plus, several others had found their way to the Counselor Corner. Each one needed something a little different, yet all were interrelated. Each was learning to strengthen their classroom culture of success.

Kris walked briskly to the supply cupboard when she spotted Dr. LaValle, sitting aloof from the others, crunching ice chunks and correcting her latest round of tests.

Yes, Trisha LaValle. The only interaction they'd had was that awkward exchange regarding Seth Gittens. She had a reputation for creating scholars and was clearly respected by all. But despite her accomplishments, there was something about her that didn't seem right. Something didn't fit. Yes, it was obvious that she was a little full of herself, but really, who didn't have some pride? Whether it came from the talk of others or that one brief exchange, something felt amiss.

Whatever it was, Kris concluded there was no doubt Dr. LaValle was, in the end, a teacher of influence. She hoped that one day their paths would cross a little closer so she could better relate to this woman of high regard.

—m—

"Just back off! You're like some crazy drill-sergeant, with a shrill voice and a fat head. Now take your witch nose, turn it around, and back up off me!"

It happened. They both knew this day would come. Their daily battles had persisted for three full weeks, and whether passive or aggressive, each battle seemed to get a little more heated. Trisha's anger had become as thick as her doctoral dissertation while her self-control had become as thin as the diploma it had won her.

And Seth knew it. At first he had taken some personal pleasure in aggravating the queen, but it had gotten old fast. To him, their battles had quickly turned from games to reality. He hated her. He hated everything about her. And today after the bell had rung and the students had left for lunch, she had kept him to discuss his missing homework. And of course, the conversation turned sour quickly. Eventually, when she had threatened to call home to give his parents "a little talking to," he lost it. She could insult him all day, but the second she messed with his family, the gloves came off.

"Back off?" retorted Trisha. "Who's the one who finally decided to lift his head off the desk, let alone actually stand up? Boy, you don't understand what you're doing. Every day you come here and give no more effort than to breathe. My standards are through this roof, and you're stuck on the bottom rung. Every day I've tried to lift you up the ladder, but every day you choose to fall back down. At some point, you're going to have to pick yourself up and climb because no one will be there to help. You'll have pushed them all away."

> From 3.5.1 – "Never demean or belittle; instead build and strengthen."

"Liar! You haven't picked me up. All I hear from you are insults. You think that helps anyone, including those brainiacks? You're a freakin' liar, and a hypocrite too. I'd rather stick that pencil in my eye before I do any work for you. Either that or jam it up your disgusting nose!"

"Silence! I will not tolerate such insubordinate garbage."

"Fine. I'm gone, witch." And with that Seth marched off, his hair swaying to the protest of his stomping shoes down the hall.

Trisha's eyes fell upon the empty door frame, blinking in time to the thudding beat of her raging heart. That wretched kid had tried to rip it out, but there it stayed, pulsating with anger still unquenched.

—∞—

Trisha stood, leaning against the exterior wall of the school, behind the bike racks. Her heart still pounded from the altercation earlier that day, and she fully intended to have the last word. She had previously learned that Seth and a younger sister walked home together, and each day they met up after school at the bike rack. So there she waited. She waited to deliver that creature a letter of reprimand in which she detailed Seth's lengthy list of misbehaviors, the standards to which she expected him to conform, and the firm consequences he could expect if immediate change did not occur.

> From 4.2.2 – "Whether [a self-centered teacher recognizes] it in themselves or not, they prioritize themselves over students."

It was Trisha's intention to simply hand him the letter and leave, without saying a word. For though she had concluded she wouldn't back down, a silent approach would avoid causing a scene, a scene that would alert others to the brewing problems in her problemless class.

Trisha tapped her heel in impatience. Several students had come and gone, each giving her an inquisitive look from either shock or intimidation at seeing a teacher at the bike racks, Dr. LaValle in particular. But no one said a word. She felt rather misplaced, but her determination to see this through prevented her retreat, no matter how awkward she felt.

As a few more students retrieved their bikes and went on their way, one young girl bid goodbye to some friends and hung back on the other side of the racks. Trisha noticed that the girl had a cheerful countenance. As she flashed a smile at a group of seventh graders passing by, Trisha detected a darling little dimple appear on one of her cheeks.

Eventually, the young girl turned just enough to notice Trisha's presence. With a polite nod and shy but sweet little smile, the girl acknowledged the unusual presence of a teacher at the racks. Intrigued, Trisha returned the smile and replied with a kind "hello."

The congenial girl seemed pleased with the reciprocated politeness, and then with all the confidence of an unassuming child, she took several steps closer to Trisha.

"Hello there! How are you today?" inquired the girl.

"Just fine, thank you. And how are you?"

"Great! I already got all my homework done during lunch so I can go to the skate park this afternoon!"

Trisha was a little surprised that such a sweet girl would spend time with skater hoodlums. "Is that so? The skate park? Why would you want to spend your free time there?"

"That's where my brother skates! He is really good. His friends are pretty good too, but I love to watch my brother. He's the best out of everyone!"

Trisha began to put two and two together. Bike rack. After school. Little girl. Skater brother. This sweet little thing must have had the unfortunate life sentence of blood relation to that skater punk she'd come here to punish. Poor thing. She probably didn't even realize how bad she had it.

"He's pretty good, huh? I bet he became good with lots of practice. Does he spend a lot of time skating?"

"Well, kind of," replied Sarah. "He does spend most of his free time skating, but he just doesn't really have much free time. He spends most of his day helping me and our two other little sisters."

Trisha paused, a little taken back by this revelation. "Helping you and your sisters? What about your parents. Why can't they help you?"

Sarah's once cheerful eyes slightly fell, revealing that this conversation was beginning to tread on sensitive ground. "My parents don't really do much, to tell you the truth. We haven't seen our dad in years. And my mom? Well, she's usually either asleep on the couch or out with some guy. We don't really see much of her either."

Trisha's heart sank. Where it was once full of anger, it now sat as empty as the door frame to her classroom at the exit of he who was the subject of her letter. Though as unanticipated as his placement in her class, Kris could now see where this was going. She hadn't considered Seth's life circumstances. She had prejudged him; she had labeled him, and he was living up to her low expectations.

"I'm so sorry to hear that, sweetheart. I bet you're glad you have a big brother to help you."

At that comment, the girl's face immediately returned to the light it was before. "Oh, yes! Seth is the best! Sometimes he teases me too much, but it's okay. He does so much for me. He even used all his savings to buy me this bike. I knew he had been working to get himself a new skateboard, but he saw how hard it was for me to walk to school every day. So on my birthday last year he took me to the store and let me pick out whatever bike I wanted. And now that I'm in sixth grade, we go to the same school, so we can ride together. But of course I'm faster on my bike than he is on his skateboard!"

> From 2.2.3 – "When [a student is] treated as the exceptional individual that they are, the cords of respect and trust will strengthen."

Trisha's heart had turned from angry to empty, and now it was filled with something quite different – compassion. As this angel continued her loving discourse, Trisha felt her whole world drastically shift. She felt the pendulum within come swinging down in haste, then arching back up to smack her in the face. What had she been doing? How could she have not seen it, considered it? This obnoxious skater kid was not what she had made him out to be. He was, in reality, a saint.

The boldly worded letter weighed heavy in her hand. It seemed to burn her flesh with both blame and shame. Feeling the sudden urge to flee, she pointed her nose down at her shoes, thanked the girl for the pleasant conversation, and hurried back toward the entrance of the school, careful not to make eye contact with any exiting student, fearful she'd have to face the source of her shame.

Trisha slowly marched toward the Counselor Corner. After her revelation at the bike racks after school, she had fled to her classroom where she tried to recover in solitude, away from anyone who'd see her in such a state of volatility. For an hour she had alternated from sitting to pacing then back again, all in a feeble effort to regain her composure. But she couldn't. How could she? She had treated this boy like an object. And not just any object, because objects can be useful; she had treated him more like a spittoon – only worthy of her discarded waste.

And as challenging as he was, Trisha now had a clear picture as to why. The game of life had dealt him the unfortunate hand of survival and parenthood at a tender age. One that young wasn't mature enough to properly care for himself, let alone three others still younger than he. Trisha had never felt any such burden, a burden that Seth was forced to brave every day. No wonder he slept in class and didn't do his homework.

Eventually her anguish propelled her to the conclusion that she needed help. And such a conclusion was not only foreign to the great Dr. LaValle, it hurt. How could others pull her up when she herself was clearly on top? However, this revelation, as painful as it was, brought with it a needed antidote to her most potent vice of vanity – humility.

"Good afternoon, Kris. Do you mind if I take a few moments of your time?" Trisha stammered as she tentatively stepped through the open doorway to the counselor's office.

"Oh my! Welcome Trisha! I'm thrilled you've come to see me." Kris stood up from behind her desk and beckoned for Trisha to sit down on one of the twin white leather chairs as she sat at her own on the other side of candy table. "To what do I owe this unexpected pleasure?"

Trisha sat for a moment, speechless, gazing downward in the same direction of her lowly heart. She didn't know what she wanted to say; all she did know, however, was that she was conflicted and needed a steady hand of help.

"Here."

Kris broke the silence with an outstretched hand holding the now familiar symbol of support, a KitKat. Trisha raised her drooped head enough to see the offering. With a deep breath of humility, she took the gift and unwrapped its contents. Kris did so with another, and the two sat quietly for a moment longer, savoring the taste of goodwill.

Feeling somewhat renewed, Trisha mustered some strength and let her heart do the talking. "Kris, I know you're new here this year. We haven't had much chance to get acquainted."

"True," Kris kindly interjected, "but I've sure heard quite a lot about you, good things, of course."

"Well, I'd say the same for you. Word has traveled fast how you've been able to help a lot of teachers. I've never seen someone come and establish her identity so quickly. It's like you've been here for years."

Kris was a little taken aback by the kind words; she hadn't pictured Trisha as the complimentary type. "That's quite kind, Trisha. Thank you. I've enjoyed my first month at East Crossroads. This school is full of great people, like you. At times I've marveled how everyone holds you in such high regard. The first person I heard about upon joining this team was the great Dr. Trisha LaValle. It must be hard to live up to such high expectations, but I have no doubt that you do."

"Yes, I'm aware of the talk, and that's what brings me to your office. I've always been one who knows what to do, one who achieves at the highest level. But I'm afraid I've got a situation right now where I've drawn a blank. I don't know what to do, and that's the scary part – I always know what to do!"

Kris responded with a conciliatory smile. She didn't know Trisha well, but it had been pretty easy to perceive that she lived with a small streak of arrogance. Such an admission was probably hard, and only served to make the problem large.

"It's Seth, isn't it?"

"Yep."

"Well, I'm not surprised he's causing some challenges. I've been keeping an eye on him and have noticed several causes for concern. I haven't worried about him as much in math with you at the helm. Has he been acting up for you too?"

"Yes. But that's not the problem." And at that, she stopped. She knew what her heart wanted to say, but her mind was preventing it. She had trained herself to hide all weakness and mask all vulnerability. The thought of saying what she needed to say swirled around in her stomach, causing a slight bit of nausea.

Seeing her hesitation, Kris's face softened and she nodded with encouragement. Her countenance seemed to say, "It's okay. You're safe here."

So, in an effort to calm her nerves, Trisha filled her lungs with the refreshing air of truth and released her thoughts slowly. Then, having inched her way to the starting line, suddenly she took off with a jolt - the sleeping, the ignoring, the raggedy hair. She sped through the first turn – the fighting, the yelling, the skater hoodie. She pushed through the second curve – his insults, her threats, his defiant departure. Then she sprinted down the homestretch – his sister, their poverty, her insidious blindness!

She stumbled through the finish line and collapsed at the strain of the race. Her head fell into the palms of her perspiring hands where her eyes added to the resident moisture. There she sat cradling her emotions as her heavy breathing gradually rescinded back to normalcy.

Ever so slowly, as delicate as a feather, Kris stood from her lone leather chair and maneuvered over to the one next to her trembling colleague. She placed her hand on Trisha's slumped back and gently stroked away the first layer of pain. The two remained silent in that position for several minutes, the concern in the one as strong as the vulnerability in the other. Trisha had revealed herself; she had actually opened up and showed the tenderness of her sentiments. And in so doing, she had pulled back her crumbling façade of vanity to prepare the way for a firmer foundation of a more beautiful, permanent structure.

Trisha raised her head up from her glistening palms. She slowly turned her red eyes to meet the caring ones looking back. Eventually, the sides of Trisha's lips creased upward, forming a small, crescent grin. Relieved, Kris's did the same. The honesty of the moment signified that Trisha's future, and subsequently those of her students, were going to be quite different from the past. A foundation of growth was beginning to take shape.

—m—

Seth peered through his shaggy hair at his reflection in the boy's bathroom mirror, his face unable to conceal the anxiety within. All day he had dreaded the thought of returning to the doctor's classroom. Yesterday's episode wasn't like their previous battles; those had all been mere firecrackers compared to this cherry bomb. He hadn't slept all night worrying about the retribution she'd be sure to inflict. *She pretty much called me garbage. And I called her a liar… and a witch! I even made fun of her nose. Oh man, how can I ever face her again?*

Seth continued to stare at his dreary reflection as the warning bell sounded for fourth period. *I wish time could just stop so I didn't have to face this. Then I could just chill at the park, skate 'till I drop, and forget about it all.*

The ring of the tardy bell roused Seth enough for his eyes to fall from his reflection in the mirror down to his gray t-shirt. Aloud, he read the black letters stretched out on top of the depiction of an elongated skateboard – "Can't We All Just Get A-Long... Board?"

He raised his head back up to meet the exhausted eyes staring back at him. With some effort, Seth forced his face into a strained grin, the smile signifying his inner surrender. *Alright man, it's now or never. And since it can't be never, it's gotta be now. Let's get this over with.*

Seth maneuvered his way through the empty halls to the math wing. Pausing just outside the classroom door, he took a deep breath, reached for the handle, and plunged inside. As quickly as his skater shoes could take him, he headed to the back of the room to his usual seat, completely avoiding any eye contact with the queen or her royal subjects.

Once seated, Seth was surprised to see a small piece of white paper folded in half sitting on his desk. Curious, he looked a little closer to see a single word written in cursive handwriting with a purple pen, "Seth."

This unanticipated note caught Seth off guard. He hadn't known what to expect, shouting, threats, the silent treatment maybe? But this certainly wasn't on the list of possibilities. *What in the world could be inside? Maybe it's more detention. Or suspension. Oh shoot, it's probably a letter to my mom! Ah, whatever it is, it can't be good.*

> From 4.2.3 – A student-centered teacher "accommodates individuals through modified assignments, tutoring, or other means, despite the additional effort necessary to do so."

Seth chanced a look up to see if Dr. LaValle would somehow reveal herself and hint at the note's contents. But there she was, slowly walking up and down the aisles as her students finished their warm up, as always. *She won't even look at me, also not a good sign.*

He looked back down. The purple cursive glared back at him with contempt, daring him to peek inside and discover his fate. *I guess it's that now or never thing again.*

"Fifteen minutes, that's all I ask. Listen and take notes for the first fifteen minutes of the lesson. When you do, you may use the pillow in the cubby beneath your chair and rest for the remainder of class. Fifteen minutes."

Huh? Seth reached underneath his chair and pulled out a small, round throw pillow. The soft, cream colored silk was soothing to the touch, wetting the young skater's appetite for some much needed slumber after his restless night. *Fifteen minutes? Really? What's up with the witch doctor? I assume if I lay on it now that it'd become a royal pillow fight pretty quick. So, fifteen minutes for some sleep… and no suspension? Yeah man, I think I can do that. Let's hope there's no trick.*

Before getting out his spiral notebook, Seth looked up at his teacher to see if this was for real. Surely, there had to be some catch. But Dr. LaValle didn't even look at him. The students had finished their warm ups and handed in their homework. So as Dr. LaValle reached for her stately baton, Seth jolted upright, flung open his notebook, checked the clock, and let his pencil fly as fast as the flashing purple before him. *That nap is going to feel especially good without her poking me.*

"He did it! He actually listened! He didn't go a second longer than fifteen minutes, but he did it!"

Kris clapped her hands together in genuine celebration of this small but monumental victory. Trisha had burst into her office right after fourth period, the gusto of her enthusiasm nearly causing Kris to drop her Caesar salad. She was so pleased to hear that their little pillow plan had worked that she then forgot about her lunch, beckoned Trisha in, and the two took some time to revel in their success.

"So, tell me what happened?"

"Well, he was a little later to class than normal. I was getting worried that he wasn't going to show up, but sure enough, about five minutes late he sneaked in and hurried back to his desk. I noticed it didn't take him very long to discover the note you had helped me with. But Kris! It was like torture to not look at him! I sneaked a peek only once or twice, and when

I did I could see him struggling to know what to do. But I was good, I let him think it through, and I let him make the decision."

"Look at you! What self-control!"

Trisha's nose perked up slightly at the compliment. "I know, right? So, when it was time for notes, I just grabbed the marker and charged onward as usual. After a minute or so I glanced back in his direction, and there he was, upright with pencil in hand taking notes! Seth! Taking notes!"

"Ah yes, the sight of success; I know that must have felt good. How'd you do the rest of the lesson? Could you focus?"

"Barely. I felt my hand shaking when writing on the board, kind of like my first year teaching, except that was nerves and this was excitement! My handwriting was terrible!"

Kris giggled at the thought of the great Dr. LaValle shaking from anything. "So, am I safe to assume he did it? He lasted the full fifteen minutes?"

"He did! I could tell that during the last few he was losing motivation. I kept looking at the clock, and that stupid thing was moving so slow! But yes, he kept going. And the second after the time had passed, he dropped his pencil and looked up at me. At that, I winked and nodded my head. He then reached for the pillow and snoozed away."

"Yes! And I bet the snoring was music to your ears!"

"Absolutely!" Trisha chuckled with delight. The two sat back in their white leather chairs, breathing in the satisfaction of the moment. Kris tossed Trisha a KitKat, and they munched while lost in thought.

Eventually, Trisha broke the silence with some pensive thinking. "You know Kris, I feel more pleased by Seth's fifteen minutes of note taking than I've ever felt about winning awards like teacher of the year."

"Well said."

"It's weird that something so small could feel so large."

Kris smiled with empathy. "It seems to me, Trisha, that you're beginning to experience the joy of, what I like to call, student-centered instruction, where the teacher makes adjustments based on the needs of individual students."

Kris paused a brief moment for Trisha to make the connection. "A student-centered teacher's methods can be quite different from the norm. "They'll first gather information, taking note of students' strengths, weaknesses, and personal challenges that may impede their progress. And then they use that information to make appropriate accommodations."

Trisha tossed the wrapper of the candy bar in a nearby trash can. "'Taking note of personal challenges.' As hard as it is to admit, it took me awhile to see those in Seth."

"Some kids are pretty good at hiding them."

"And some teachers are pretty good at overlooking them," replied Trisha, dropping her head slightly.

As perceptive as a mother, Kris picked up on Trisha's self-depreciating thoughts. To a certain extent, Kris felt that such could actually be good for her. Trisha was certainly not a bad person nor a neglectful teacher, but a small serving of humble pie might be just what she needed. And yet, a foundation of humility would be useless unless upon it was built the framework and fixtures of student-centered instruction. Yes, Trisha's pride had been sufficiently stripped down. It was time to build her back up.

"And that being true, Trisha, the good news is that such teachers can change. Is change hard? Of course. We get in our habits and routines which create feelings of safety and normalcy. We like that, so change can be intimidating. But in the end, I firmly disagree with the old saying 'you can't teach an old dog new tricks.' That's complete fallacy. People change every day! All they need is to see a new way and have enough desire to put it to practice."

Trisha took note of the saying and tried to forget the fact that she had recently used it to insult Paul just the other day. "So, how do you get that desire?" Trisha paused mid-thought to properly place the answer to her rhetorical question. "Experiences. Eye opening experiences."

Kris knowingly nodded, understanding the meaning behind Trisha's words. "Which brings us back to Seth, doesn't it?"

"Exactly. I don't know if I would have ever tried anything different with Seth had I not learned more about his home life. That poor boy is a slave in the form of a skater. He needs someone to look at his situation and cut him some slack, someone to make accommodations."

"Now," Kris persisted, "he still needs to be held to a high standard, but…"

"…but a high standard that is unique to him," interrupted Trisha, finishing Kris's thought.

"Like fifteen minutes of note taking."

"Now that was brilliant! While I wouldn't think of lowering the standard for my other students, fifteen minutes was just right for him. It made him stretch, but it was doable," Trisha summarized.

"And now that he's experienced some success, you can build on it from there."

"Perfect! But I could use some more ideas. What else have you got?"

Kris chuckled at Trisha's earnest request. Yet though she was eager to be of assistance, Kris caught herself just in time. She could foresee how the situation itself was going to be the best teacher of all, much better than anything she could say. And though Kris would have loved to spew out all she knew about student-centered instruction, somehow she knew that it would be better learned when experienced. So, she resisted the lecture, knowing Trisha would get there soon enough.

"Hold on now, Trisha! You're such a wonderful teacher, I'm sure you've got all the ideas right there within you. We just need to collaborate and see if we can pull them out. Here's some scratch paper. Let me ask you a few questions."

Trisha hurried to the teachers' lounge to grab her lunch after spending all her break with Kris. Lucky for her, she had prep fifth period.

"Greetings Trish! Did you come here to sneak extra supplies when no one's looking? I'd think admin would frown on such deplorable actions."

Unlucky for her, Paul had prep fifth period too.

"No. Just half of an egg salad sandwich from home. I'd give the other half to Mr. Phippen, but it's probably not necessary. My track record speaks for itself." Though not really in the mood for banter, Trisha couldn't help herself. What was it that Kris just said about old dogs and new tricks?

"You're referring to your distinguished track record of snobbery, no doubt?"

Returning to the exit with lunch in hand, Trisha resisted. She fought back at the habit, now having some motivation to change. "You know Paul, it's not worth it. Enjoy your bologna."

Trisha exited the lounge, her nose pointing upward for a different reason this time. *Change. I can do this.*

The next day, Trisha found herself pacing up and down the rows of desks during the warm up a little faster than usual. The clacks of her heels emphasized the beating of her impatient heart. She had such great success yesterday, but today was another day. She fully understood that her pillow experiment could backfire at any moment. Seth could just grab for the pillow right away, refuse to work, or skip class altogether. All these options seemed just as likely as her next plan working. They needed to build on yesterday's progress, not use it as fuel for a fight.

The minutes for the warm up ticked on with no sign of Seth; his empty desk called out for companionship. Yet at the ring of the timer, in he walked as if it had taken the place of the tardy bell. As he stumbled back to his desk, Trisha sensed that something seemed to be different, but she couldn't tell what it was. His scraggly hair peeked out from underneath his hoodie, as always. His jeans had holes in the knees, as always. He had some ridiculous skater slogan slapped across his chest, as always. All seemed in order, but Trisha felt the vibe that something wasn't right.

As the class proceeded, Trisha's attention narrowed to the back of the room. Seth slumped over in his chair, his hunched shoulders heavy with some new unknown burden. Peering past the tangled strands of blond hair drooped over his eyes, he stared at another note with purple lettering requesting his attention. He didn't touch it. He didn't move at all. He just sat there staring at it, the wheels in his head doing all the moving that his body refused to do.

At the respectful nudging of a student on the front row, Trisha awoke from her trance to notice that the class had finished grading the warm up and passing in their homework. They now sat ready to press onward to the lesson. With a belabored creak, Trisha forced her heels to move her mind from the back of the room and her body to the white board. As she reached for her purple marker, she took one glance back to see Seth still frozen in position, the note untouched, his shoulders slumped as he bore the pain of an unfortunate life.

Trisha knew that she needed to do something, but she didn't want to draw unnecessary attention to the delicate situation. She concluded that she just needed him to look up at her, but his eyes were fixated in place. And if she called out his name, his defenses were sure to arise.

After a few minutes into the lesson, Trisha arrived at an example problem to be worked on the board. An idea surfaced. Instead of modeling it herself as usual, she asked if any of the students would be interested in coming up and doing so themselves. A wave of disbelief rippled across the class. What? Slow down note taking? A student write on the board? The unheard of request caught everyone off guard, which brought all eyes up front – including Seth's.

One student shyly raised her hand. As she made her way up to the unchartered waters, Trisha caught Seth's eyes. Locked together for a fleeting moment, Trisha gave half a smile and an encouraging nod toward the note on his desk. Seth looked down. He hesitantly picked it up, weighed it in his hand, then looked back up at his teacher. The look in his troubled eyes seemed to shout the poignant question, why? Why are you all of the sudden helping me? Can't you see my burden? I've got more important things to consider than geometry. Can't you see that?

Trisha smiled and nodded again. Whether due to her encouragement or his teenage curiosity, Trisha didn't know, but Seth looked back down at the note, filled his lungs, and opened it.

"Again, fifteen minutes and the pillow's yours. I've reduced your homework assignment tonight to just the odds. I've arranged for you to complete it in the Counselor Corner right after school. Your sister already knows you'll be late. Complete the assignment, and the pillow option will again be available tomorrow."

Journal Entry – October 5

Check me out! I'm journaling! Kris has been telling me to jot down my thoughts and do some reflecting in written form. I kept telling her my stack of papers to grade is calling, but how can I argue with the results she's helped me produce? She's been a great help and support, so here we go.

It has been just a few days since I learned about Seth's home life. That knowledge really shook me up, to say the least. I had been so intent on forcing my will upon him, like all my other students, that I failed to see I was doing more harm than good. But now I've got him paying attention in class (if only for a short time) and completing his homework (though only a portion). And as hard as it is for me to deviate from my normal routine and standards, doing so has pointed Seth in a better direction.

But now, here's the kicker. Not only am I writing in a journal, but I'm also going to complete an assignment! I'm the one who is used to dishing those out; this receiving of them is a little new.

So Kris and I had a discussion on student-centered instruction, which is really what I'm trying to do with Seth. She gave me the assignment to define it in my own words, along with two other methods – lesson-centered and self-centered. We've yet to discuss those last two, but I bet I can give it try; I am a doctor after all.

Lesson-Centered Instruction: *The primary focus is to deliver a quality lesson instead of producing a quality product. This method engages students in the process of the learning activity while neglecting the activity's very purpose. It seeks after the "wow-factor" more than student achievement. Also, it does not consider the learning needs of individual students because it cares more for the positive reaction of the whole.*

Self-Centered Instruction: *The primary focus is to teach in a manner that fulfills the objectives and needs of the teacher, sometimes at the expense of students. A self-centered teacher's mentality is often that teaching is "just a job." This method doesn't consider each class's unique needs, and it avoids making individual accommodations. These teachers often cut corners, teach methodically, and are selfish with their time.*

Student-Centered Instruction: *The primary focus is to guide students to achieve according to their individual circumstances, prioritizing student success above all else. It tailors lessons to class needs and accommodates individuals. It is willing to flex from lesson plans if assessment so dictates. These teachers are unselfish with their time and are willing to sacrifice their own needs to help individual students.*

Now, this is a reflection, so I better reflect. As hard as it is to say, I've trended toward self-centered instruction for much of my career. I believe deep down my goals have been good as I've worked to help my students succeed at the highest level, but I must painfully admit that my motives and methods have often been a little selfish. I'm just starting to learn, but I see good progress. I see the path of change just ahead of me.

Boy, who knew a rebellious skater kid could have such an influence?

Empowered

—∞—

Seth settled in for another well-earned rest on Dr. LaValle's throw pillow. The smoothness of the silk felt cool on his skin after growing warm from concentration. He was now several days into this new arrangement: fifteen minutes of notes, time in the Counselor Corner, half the homework, and the culmination of a short nap as a reward. He didn't know what to think about it. He liked the softer standards, but he didn't like the work, even when reduced. He liked the absence of the daily battles, but he was unsure of his teacher's motives. *Why the sudden change? And what does she want from me anyway? Is this just a trick to keep me quiet until the end of the year?*

With his head planted on the pillow, Seth gazed down at his shirt. He studied the cartoon depiction of an old man with baggy jeans, skater shoes, and long gray hair flowing out from his backwards hat, catching air on his skateboard. Underneath the soaring board read the words, "Keep on Rollin.'" *Yeah, right.*

Seth clenched his fists in anger. *Who does this chick think she is? She doesn't know me. Here she is cuttin' back on my homework and throwin' me pillows; does she really think that helps? My life's a freakin' disaster, man. No parents. No time. I'm sittin' here worryin' 'bout how to get my sisters to bed safe away from mom's loser boyfriend. And I gotta figure out how to scrounge up some money so they can have lunch at school tomorrow. Half the homework? Please! How 'bout a job?*

Seth pulled his hood down over his eyes, intent on concealing the watery evidence of his escaping inner anguish. As strong as he was, this past week had produced tears more often than before. A new trial had surfaced, and its negative effects were churning inside like a storm.

Now, Seth had lived enough adult experiences to understand bad from worse. For instance, little food – bad / no food – worse. Addict mother – bad / stalker boyfriend – worse. One would think that constant exposure to such horrendous circumstances would have hardened Seth to the point that a stolen bicycle would be meaningless.

However, that was indeed the source of Seth's extra agony. While in school, someone had come to the racks, broken off the cheap lock (it being the only one he could afford), and ran off with his little sister's bike. The bike for which he'd saved up for nearly a year, the bike Sarah needed to make the long trek to school. It was gone. Months of sacrifice, gone, and no way to bring it back. With his eyes still closed and his fists clenched, Seth's mind remained locked in on his burdens which dragged him deeper and deeper into his misery. His fury continued to swirl and swell within.

It had been complete coincidence that the incident of the stolen bike had occurred near the same time frame as Dr. LaValle's revelation. And it only added to Seth's confusion. She had reached out, so any decent person would reach back. And that's what he had done. He took notes. He did his homework. His teacher offered him generous accommodations, but it irked him that her generosity was also the cause of more demands being placed on his troubled shoulders. Sure, he was doing half the work as everyone else, but that was double anything he had previously done. And while he had felt a personal sense of accomplishment he hadn't experienced at school since before his dad left years ago, it was bothering him to have his attention diverted away from where it needed to be. His sisters needed him, but he was being tugged away by some royal doctor in high heels.

I don't know how much more of this I can take. I've got to use my energy to make money for a new bike for Sarah. I don't have time for this lady. I don't have time for these stupid shapes! I need food! I need money!

As the clock wound toward the concluding minutes of class, Seth's inner storm swelled toward a ferocious climax. The blackened clouds of his thoughts thrust his emotions into a frenzy, threatening an involuntary thunderous release through his trembling jaw. He caught his breath and held it, making every effort to calm the thrashing winds. The clock ticked toward the dismissal bell, yet it was still several minutes away from releasing the mounting pressure. *What do I do? Why me?*

The swell of the storm continued to build until it finally pushed forward to a fragment of release, but not by the ring of a bell or the shout of his voice. Instead, silently the rains poured down out from underneath the loneliness of the hood, soaking the silk pillow underneath.

Empowered

Journal Entry – October 19

It has been a few weeks now since I started providing accommodations for Seth. And I'll be honest, my initial reaction to some of Kris's ideas was skepticism at best. A pillow? Really? But there he was, complying with my every wish that first week.

And it has been intriguing to observe the positive changes occurring with my other students as well. Granted I'm only a few weeks in, but I've begun to change my overall approach a little. Kris keeps talking to me about individualizing the instruction and considering the needs of each student. I'm still trying to figure out exactly what that looks like – I've got over 100 students to consider – but I'm beginning to pick up some things.

For instance, last Thursday I noticed my students really struggling with proofs. Where my lesson plans called for me to move on, I decided to slow down a bit and take another day to practice. Also, just yesterday I could tell from Haley's homework that she still wasn't grasping it, so I had her stop by before school this morning for some tutoring. It might take a couple more sessions, but she's already making good progress.

> From 4.2.3 – A student-centered teacher is "willing and able to flex from lesson plans according to student needs."

To be honest, between these small shifts and really working with Seth, I'm having a lot of fun. Granted, it's an increase to my work load, but I'm already beginning to see how student-centered instruction, as Kris calls it, can produce better results than my traditional methods. I'm excited to see where this goes.

Now, another note about Seth. I'm worried. Yes, he's made great progress since he first moved in, but something's not right. I began to sense it not long ago as I was just about ready to increase his minimum standards. He began to push back again. Nothing quite like before, but he's been arriving a little later, writing a little sloppier, arguing a little more, etc. My first instinct was that it was just his old habits bringing him back down, but now I'm not so sure. I can't put my finger on it, but there's obviously something else wrong, something new.

So, I've kept his standards the same, fifteen minutes of notes and half the homework, and I'm just hoping to see some more of that progress that he initially made. He's such a bright kid. As hard as he tries to hide it, I can see past that skater façade. He's a bright kid in a terrible situation. And with each passing day, whatever this new challenge is, it seems to be dragging him lower and lower. I fear I'm losing him. But what else can I do?

"Fifteen minutes late, Kris! I didn't dare call the office because he'd be sure to hate me and regress back to where we started. But I knew he was at school today, and I didn't know what to do. Eventually, I sent out another student to look for him. He found Seth in the bathroom, just staring at himself in the mirror. He's becoming so reclusive again. He's shutting himself back in. He's just... well, he's..."

Kris waited silently as Trisha caught her breath while straining to pick up the pieces of her fragmented thoughts. Kris noticed how her friend's eyes scanned the walls of the office, as if searching for words to accurately reflect her inner fears, those wordless mental shapes only fully understood as a visual.

Catching Trisha's eyes, Kris gently prodded her onward with an encouraging nod. Trisha eventually broke the stare as her gaze fell to her feet. Never quite finding the right words, she settled for simplicity.

"Kris, I'm losing him."

Kris gazed at her dejected colleague, feeling a twist of concern coupled with pride. The concern she felt belonged to that of the student in question, not for Trisha. She was strong. She was learning. All of this was providing her great opportunity for personal growth, and Kris was proud of the strides she was making. However, it was clear that Seth was going downhill fast. He hadn't shown up in the Counselor Corner after school the last two days, and Kris was aware of behavior issues in his other classes as well. This boy needed help, and he needed it fast.

"Just look at you, Trisha. Look how much you care. That boy's well-being has become your top priority, something I'm not sure you could have said just a few weeks ago."

"True. But it really isn't getting us anywhere, is it?"

"It may seem like that now, sure, but we're not done yet. Right? Though it looks like we've lost some ground, all's not lost. We can still do some good for this boy."

"Anymore tricks?" Trisha inquired with a hint of sarcasm. "I think the pillow has lost its appeal."

"Tricks? I may have a few strategies to consider. But let's first step back and look at the big picture. There are some guiding principles we can apply to this situation."

With her head still hanging low, Trisha's eyes looked up and across the room at Kris, her expression showing that humility had continued to supplant her vanity. As her heart changed, so did her motives. As her motives changed, so did her actions.

> From 4.3 – "It is impossible to outline concrete [applications of student-centered instruction] that could be universally applied. In fact, it shouldn't even be attempted, for doing so would ultimately fail at least some small sector of students."

"Okay Kris, I'm listening." At Trisha's expression of willingness, Kris reached into the drawer of the candy table. Trisha waved her hands in protest.

"No, Kris! No more candy. I'm sure I've put on a few pounds because of our visits."

"Oh? What makes you think I was going to give this to you?"

"Because you always do."

"Oh. True. But not this time. Instead, I want you to consider this KitKat as if it were a method of instruction in your classroom."

"Instead of a method of hip expansion?" Trisha teased.

"If you say so!" Kris then flipped the candy bar in the air and caught it with a swipe of her hand. "This candy bar can represent the three different methods of instruction we've discussed. If we're going to reach Seth, our best chance is through student-centered instruction."

"In case you haven't noticed, that's what I've been trying."

Kris ignored the pessimism. "Let's first take lesson-centered instruction. How could this KitKat represent that method?"

Trisha wasn't in the mood for riddles. "It teaches math; you know, one bar plus one bar. Kris, I don't know!"

"Take a look at the wrapper," Kris persisted. "To a lesson-centered teacher, it's all about the presentation. They make the wrapper as shiny and attractive as possible. And while their whole focus is on the show, what then is neglected?"

Trisha sat a little straighter, beginning to understand the analogy. "The candy bar."

"Yes, the substance itself. The irony is that they rarely get to the very thing they're trying to sell."

Trisha stared across the room at the candy in Kris's hand, contemplating the impact of the analogy yet struggling to understand how it related to Seth. She felt she needed concrete ideas to turn him around, not big picture philosophy.

"Now, what about self-centered instruction? How could this method be represented by the KitKat?"

Trusting her friend, Trisha tried to swallow her irritation and made an effort to answer the question. "I suppose they'd save the candy for themselves."

"Exactly. These teachers are so concerned about themselves and their own time, happiness, or success that they fail to pursue the true joy of giving it all away."

Trisha sat back in her chair, crossed her legs, and rested her weary head by holding it up by her chin. She tapped a heel as her mind raced. After several moments, a hint of a smile broke through and her eyes revealed her understanding. Trisha raised her head to meet the friendly eyes of her mentor, wordlessly expressing her comprehension and willingness for more.

"Lastly, what about student-centered instruction?"

Trisha immediately responded in a confident tone. "It's given away. The KitKat is completely given to the student."

"No."

Trisha's eyes flashed in surprise. How could her answer be wrong? Seth needed her; he needed the entire candy bar. How could a student-centered teacher reserve some of the substance for herself?

Kris let the impact of the disagreement sink in, allowing Trisha to feel the full weight of its meaning. For she knew that the next lesson would be the most significant of all. Indeed, Kris herself was being student-centered, withholding the full KitKat until the moment in which it would produce the greatest impact.

Sensing Trisha's readiness, Kris began to slowly unwrap the substance within. "Trisha, if you truly want Seth to experience success, you cannot simply give it to him. He must earn it. Candy earned tastes better than candy given. You must show it to him. You must tell him how good it is. You must show him the path whereby he himself can obtain it, but it is he that must walk that path. Student-centered instruction is placing the candy at the appropriate distance, and then walking with him, side by side, until he reaches it."

At that, Trisha's eyes followed Kris's hand as she set the KitKat on the farthest edge of the table. Clearly a vote of confidence, Trisha understood how the placement communicated Kris's belief in her ability to walk the distance, no matter how far.

Trisha uncrossed her legs, and planting both heels firmly on the ground, she stood and walked around the table and picked up the chocolate metaphor. She then took a step back, unwrapped it, broke it in half, and reached out to give a bar to Kris.

"And surely, there is still some reward for such a generous friend."

Journal Entry – October 22

What am I doing wrong? Seth totally refused to take notes today. I eventually whispered a few words of encouragement near the end of class, and he just stood up and stormed out. And sure enough, he never even showed up at the Counselor Corner after school to do his homework. By the time I made it out to the bike racks, he and his sister had already left.

I don't know what else to do… I've accommodated everything I can think of… I've cut him slack in so many of ways… Everything is wrong… He was doing so well, but now he's falling off a cliff… It wasn't supposed to happen like this.

I've seriously contemplated calling state authorities to intervene. And though there are laws and policies I'm obliged to follow, I don't know if I have enough concrete information for that to do any good. Luckily, Kris is aware, so I'm not fighting this alone.

Maybe it's time for us to have a sit down talk. I haven't wanted to address it head on for fear that he'd become defensive and lash back, which is exactly what happened today. I don't want to drive him away, but what else can I do?

"Who are you to tell me what to do? You don't know me! The only reason you ever see my face is because they force me in here! I've got more important things to do. This class is worthless. You! You're worthless!"

It was going the way Trisha had expected but not how she had hoped. It was several days after Seth had stormed out, and just when Trisha thought he wasn't going to come, he stormed in. His dark, sullen face announced more clearly than his black "Sk8 or Die" hoodie that he was in no mood for math. He slammed down his backpack, crumpled up the note on his desk, threw the pillow across the room, and thumped down his head, a few scraggly strands of blond hair poking out from underneath the hood.

Trisha froze. All her tender feelings of inadequacy flushed to the surface like a clogged drain; the threat of them overflowing was just as frightening as the tears they'd bring along. Should she address him? No, he'll fight back. Should she ignore him? No, he'll keep getting worse. Trisha felt trapped, lost in thick fog without a light.

Eventually a girl in the second row, sensing her teacher's plight, raised her hand and asked for help. Thus breaking Trisha's stupor, she was able to help the girl and continue on with the lesson. However, Trisha knew continuing was only masking the problem, leaving the 800 pound gorilla dormant while attending to the others.

Seth stayed as such throughout the day's lesson, with only the occasional shift of the body or sniff of the nose to confirm his presence. As the time for the dismissal bell lurched near, Trisha's anxiety rose. She had concluded over the course of the lesson that the time had come to confront him. He'd probably yell at her. He'd probably insult her. Yet she hoped that exposing the wound would provide the opportunity for healing. Yes, she'd ask him to stay after class, rip off the bandage, and hope for the best. Each tock of the second hand was like an upward tick of her blood pressure.

"Seth, you can insult me all you want if it makes you feel better," Trisha calmly replied to Seth's outburst, "but in the end, I'm just here to help. I want to help you however I can."

"Help me? Do you think making me stay longer in this horrible classroom helps me? Do you think making me stay at school any longer than I have to, helps me? Oh boy, she gave me a pillow… how *helpful*. Please, lady. Do you really want to help me? Then, leave me alone!"

Seth's words rung loudly in Trisha's ears as he stomped from the room and down the hall, each footstep a resounding exclamation point. From the confines of her class, she stared at the diminishing figure and her dwindling hope quickly disappearing down the hall.

Vanity. There it stands, smooth and refined where visible yet jagged and tactless everywhere else. Its whole purpose, the entirety of its existence, is to bring notice to itself. It boldly shouts its accomplishments while softly denying its folly. It treats the success of another as a threat, a danger to its own rise and nobility. Vanity. It pushes away the very people it is dutifully striving to attract, the consequence of which is forced friendliness at best and self-alienation at worst.

Compassion. There it stands in stark contrast to its flamboyant neighbor. Its only intent for self-presentation is to better serve its associates. It perceives anxiety and quickly moves to alleviate the cause. It's more content to be an exuberant audience than the star on stage. It prefers the coaching box to the gold medal platform. Compassion. It is kind, optimistic, and empathetic. It attracts new friends without realizing how, the result of which is a better world.

> From 2.2.2 – "One must be on higher ground to lift another up."

Trisha looked around at the effects of the gloomy, winter's afternoon before her. The clouds hovered low and the snow piled high. A few passers-by tiptoed through the watery slush on the sidewalks looping around East Crossroads. It was that awkward phase between winter and fall where the snow didn't know if it should accumulate or dissipate, so it did neither. The plowed piles around the edges of the parking lot glistened in confusion, while the remains on the street slushed about in stubborn independence.

The queen had slipped outside just before the dismissal bell, leaving her wand and her pride behind. After her scene with Seth earlier that day, she had concluded that there was nothing to do but pick up her heart, dust if off, and give it away. So there she stood, leaning up against the wall behind the bike racks, not knowing what she'd say but knowing she must say something.

Currently, her primary fear was the empty rack before her. Had they already left? With no more bike, did they depart through some other exit?

Had she missed them? Perhaps. Yet, her compassion enlarged her determination; she'd stay until sure.

At the ring of the dismissal bell, the school erupted into action. Flurries of students broke free from the building and floated about like the beginnings of an early winter storm. Trisha observed how the students seemed to flutter together in pods of varying size and appearance. Off to the right were the athletes, pushing and laughing like thunderous hail. To the left were some sixth grade girls who whispered and giggled like soft morning snowflakes as they crossed the street. Just ahead the cheerleaders blew about, radiant and sure. Near the doors clustered some studious kids, many of them her own geometry students. She spied flurries of skaters, preppies, nerds and all.

Her eyes fell back to observe the scene in its entirety. These were the students of East Crossroads Middle School. Each had their own challenges. Each had their own fears. Though each conformed to look like their peers, each was as unique on the inside as the falling flakes of snow. And as Trisha leaned back, she smiled at the understanding of the great trust they put in her, this unique burden to be a tool of influence, however small, in each of their individual lives.

"Hi there, Dr. LaValle!"

Trisha awoke from her contemplation to see a bright smile accented by an adorable little dimple. There stood Sarah, Seth's darling little sister, looking up at her with the naivety of a toddler and the confidence of a professional.

"Good afternoon. It's Sarah, right?"

"Yes siree! Whatcha doin' out here in the cold?"

"I was actually hoping to find your brother. Do you two still meet here after school?"

"Yes again! But I always beat him here; he's so slow!"

Trisha released a small chuckle, smitten with the girl's infectious charm. "And I bet you're pretty fast! But do you think you'd win if he came straight out instead of going to the Counselor Corner to do his homework?"

"Of course I would! And yet, he hasn't been there for several days anyway. He's needed the extra time."

Trisha cocked her head to the side, the puzzled look on her face communicating to the girl her inquiry as to why. Sarah bowed her head a little, then responded with the blunt honesty uniquely possessed by children.

"My bike got stolen."

Instinctively, Trisha tried to step backward, but she was impeded by the wall upon which she still leaned. "Stolen? The one he bought for you? How? When?"

"About two weeks ago. Seth had spent all his money on the bike, so he could only afford a real cheap lock. During school, someone came and broke it off."

"Oh my! I'm sorry to hear that."

"Me too! So, now I walk with Seth all the way home. And I try to keep up, but he's always in a hurry!"

"Why is that?"

Sarah looked around as if to make sure no one was listening. "We've gotta take care of our little sisters. Seth's always out trying to make money, you know, shoveling driveways and doin' odd jobs at the warehouse. He uses most of that for food for us, but you know what?" Sarah leaned in, shielding her mouth as she whispered with excitement. "I think he's saving up again! My birthday is in a couple months, and I think he's gonna get me another bike!"

As Sarah clapped her hands together with delight, Trisha braced herself against the racks. So that was the problem! She had suspected something was wrong, something new thwarting Seth's progress. And though he had admirably cared for his family for years, the burden of such a setback must have been unbearable. To an adult, it would have felt like a stolen car or a wiped out savings account. He'd worked for months, and the result was now a waste, a waste with nothing but a cheap broken lock to show for it. No matter the amount of courage and resilience, this must have proved devastating.

"You! What are you doing here?"

Startled by the interruption, Trisha looked up in surprise to see Sarah's older brother standing to the side, fists clenched. While the two had been conversing, Seth had slowly sloshed his way to the racks, having taken his time under the burden he was forced to bear. Eventually arriving at the routine meeting place, he couldn't contain a tirade of anger at the sight of his hated teacher chatting it up with his little sister.

"Hello Seth," breathed Trisha. "I was wanting to finish our earlier conversation. And this time, I was hoping a little more calmly."

"Didn't I tell you to leave me alone? Now you're here just hangin' out with my little sister? What part of alone don't you understand?"

> From 4.2.3 – A student-centered teacher's "priorities place students above themselves."

"Seth, I understand you're angry, but let us talk for a moment. I'm just here to help."

Seth clenched his backpack and walked behind his sister, placing his hands on her shoulders. "Yeah, I know. We already went over this. You want to help, but you can't!"

Gently pushing Sarah forward, Seth began leading her away. Trisha took a step forward and reached out with her quivering hand and shaky voice. She whispered, "And why not? Can't you tell I care? I understand it's hard, Seth, I really do. Now let me help you."

Seth stopped, his back still to his teacher. Without turning to face her, he grunted, "Understand? You don't understand nothin'."

Trisha sensed an opportunity. She stepped forward and around to face both brother and sister. She bent down and took Sarah by the hands, smiling with all the sincerity she felt within. Then, while still looking into the young girl's eyes, she spoke firmly.

"Yes. Yes I do understand."

She then raised herself to her full stature and met Seth's penetrating gaze with a compassionate one of her own. She opened her mouth and related the story as she understood it from the beginning. His defiance and laziness. Her frustration and stubbornness. Her visit to the racks. Sarah's revelation. Her change of heart. His progress and subsequent decline. Her desire to help yet not knowing how.

All the while Seth stood still, stone-faced and motionless. If he understood his teacher's story, he gave no sign of it.

"So you see Seth, I do understand. Perhaps not the depth of your struggles, but I understand, at least, their existence. I understand that geometry isn't your top priority, and that's okay. But I want to help. No, I can't give you money, a new bike, or a job. I can't be a mother or a counselor. But I can be a friendly face. I can be a good listener if you ever need to talk, and I can provide a safe place for you to forget about life, if only for fifty minutes. So yes, I do understand and I do want to help, however small my help may be."

And still, Seth stood motionless, concealing whatever feelings may have been churning inside. Trisha looked down at Sarah, wordlessly pleading for assistance. And then, exasperated at his stubbornness, Sarah turned around to face her brother. She gazed up at him with a stern look of reprimand. The contemptuous stare lingered for several long moments. And then, with a sudden burst of energy, Sarah cocked back her elbows and released her childish reproach with a furious push to his gut.

Trisha jerked back in surprise. Sarah did too, a bit fearful of the probable oncoming consequence. They both looked up at Seth, whose strong upper body had barely moved at the strike of his sister's puny arms. His eyes made their way to his teacher, then back to the little girl standing in front of her. First, he furrowed his brow. Then, he tilted his head. And finally, a twinge of a smile escaped his lips.

"You call that a push? Those twig arms of yours could wear Fruit Loops as bracelets!"

At that, Sarah charged and playfully pushed him again. And again, he didn't move. The two erupted in laughter at the humor of this angel acting so out of character. Then with a chuckle, Seth nudged her back, picked up her backpack, and took a few steps toward home.

Just before crossing the street which separated the school from his world, his teacher from himself, Seth stopped and turned back to face her, the high and mighty Dr. LaValle, she who had journeyed down to his level and offered a hand of fellowship.

"Fifteen minutes?"

Trisha's heart leapt. There stood the skater, he who had tormented her into change. He whose defiance was a result of circumstances beyond his control and yet instigated her newly found compassion.

"Fifteen minutes."

Chapter Five Author's Note

There are students like Seth in countless classrooms, students who struggle in the mainstream system and stand in need of an advocate. Divorce, disability, depression, and hordes of other circumstances blunt their individual progress. Yet the number of Seths in the world pale in comparison to the hosts of average, everyday students who are just as special and just as unique. They too need our care and concern. They too need our individualized instruction.

There are also teachers like Trisha in numerous classrooms. Despite her obvious arrogant tendencies, Trisha is a good teacher. She's organized, professional, thorough, and holds her students to high expectations. Our profession is filled with teachers just as dedicated and just as diligent, who, like Trisha, can at times become lost in the distractions of some other priority. It's easy to do. We have lives outside the classroom (despite what our students might think). We have our own weaknesses and stresses (despite our efforts to overcome them). And there does exist a line where school ends and our personal lives begin. However, we must not justify away any neglectful action, or mis-action, at the expense of our students. They deserve our very best, even if our very best may occasionally extend past a forty-hour work week.

Thus, teachers are faced with the monumental task of individualizing instruction for groups of thirty or more students. That's a thirty to one ratio. Is that really the expectation? How are we supposed to do that? What was that about a forty-hour work week?

The reality is that in our current educational system, one to one is simply unattainable. However, we mustn't justify away that which we can attain. Teachers can use the resources given them according to their unique situation and apply the principles of student-centered instruction in all they do. By first eliminating wasted time, then assessing needs, and finally adjusting operations in accordance with all four principles of culture creating, teachers can meet the needs of the majority of students within the normal flow of instruction. Expect much, build trust, reinforce the good, and teach in a dynamic, student-centered manner; this will enable the success of most.

However, it is with others like Seth, those with more unique needs, that we have the best opportunity to do the greatest good. Ensuring proper development for these students will not be accomplished through a routine checklist. Teachers have at their fingertips a world of scientific research to help with struggles from bullying to ADHD to depression. We must be diligent in our own learning and vigilant to overcome our own weaknesses to be an instrument for growth and success for these students. Often times, it is the largest challenges that yield the most satisfying results.

Questions to Consider – Your Journal Entry #4

1. In what ways have I approached teaching in a lesson-centered way? Self-centered? What results have these approaches yielded for my students?

2. In what ways have I approached teaching in a student-centered way? What results has this yielded for my students?

3. Both in and out of class time, how can I change my approach to become more student-centered?

Chapter Six

The Crossroads Traversed

Journal Entry – January 3

"Work hard, play hard." That motto has been all too true this year. I've enjoyed reflecting on the first few months of school during this "play hard" Christmas break. The first semester, with a new position at a new school, has certainly required a lot of hard work. And though challenging, it has also been thoroughly enjoyable.

School starts back up tomorrow, and as anxious as I am to get back to my students, honestly, I'm equally anxious to get back to my colleagues. Who could have predicted that I'd be spending as much time as I do with teachers? I certainly never intended it to happen, it just sort of did on its own.

And I must say how impressed I am with this staff. Yes, they have their strengths and weakness, but by and large they've been completely teachable and willing to try new things. And look where it has gotten them! Take Alex for instance. His intentions were pure, he was just going about it the wrong way. And Trisha's as fine a teacher as I've ever met, but she just needed a little redirection back to the individual. And what could I say about Sheri? That spit fire has all the natural ability and ambition she'll ever need; she was just so new and raw. And of course there's Paul. It took him a little longer to crack than the others, but look at him now. He's on the cusp of a new career.

I could certainly mention others, all of whom have been equally as inspirational to me as I hope I've been to them. All they needed were a few guiding principles I've been fortunate to pick up along the way, and they took care of the rest.

—⁂—

Lunch in hand, Kris stepped through the door of the teachers' lounge on the first day back from Christmas break. Immediately, the energy in the room stopped her in her tracks. She scanned the lounge, taking in the scene as a whole. And what a pleasant image to behold! The crowd of teachers bustling about with rays of cheerfulness seemed, to Kris, like a beautiful painting. The brightness of the canvas was more vibrant than anything the stretch of florescent bulbs on the ceiling could ever produce.

"Oh, excuse me, Kris." Lost in contemplation, Kris had forgotten that she was still standing just inside the doorway, blocking its passage.

"Oh no, excuse me, Mr. Phippen" replied Kris as she stepped to the side. Her eyes followed the lanky, young assistant principal to a lively table, where he promptly grabbed a seat and joined the conversation. A few other sets of eyes from the same table noticed Kris still standing alone, and they beckoned her to join them. She smiled in return and obliged their request.

"Well there she is! Grab a seat Kris. How was your break?"

"Wonderful! Thanks for asking. What about you guys? Any fun stories to tell?"

Alex was the first to respond. "We traveled south to see family for a few days. It was nice to get away, but even nicer to come back. There's nothing quite like family time in your own home."

"Ah yes, a little vacation from vacation," Kris replied. "I know how that feels. What about you, Sheri? This was your first Christmas vacation as a full time teacher. What did you do?"

"Everything! Where do I even start? I first visited my parents for a few days. We went to the movies, ate out a few times, and, oh yeah, we went to that new museum. Have you guys been there yet? It's incredible! I spent hours at this exhibit that was, like, totally full of…"

"…Whoa, slow down there racer," interrupted Paul. Yes, his priorities had changed but his personality stayed as strong as his bowling ball. "You're doing that mind-moving-faster-than-your-mouth thing again."

"Hey now, at least the wheels in her mind are still young enough to turn that fast," teased Trisha. "Yours creak as bad as the gutter after your last game!"

The group burst into laughter at the good-natured banter between these once fierce rivals. They'd never formally called a truce, so the jokes flew as often as ever, but the newfound friendly intent had turned the uppercuts into love taps.

"You'll be happy to know I averaged 230 over the break, and… AND, I almost finished the crossword puzzle at the back of my bowling magazine. How do you like those creaky wheels now, little Miss Trish?"

The jovial conversation stretched on for several minutes as the colleagues enjoyed their reunion. After a few more stories and some harmless teasing, Paul redirected the conversation. "So, what's on the docket for the rest of the year? What are you guys looking forward to in semester two?"

"A second chance!" Sheri and Alex blurted simultaneously.

The two smiled at their impromptu duet. Alex then nodded for Sheri to elaborate, knowing he wouldn't be able to get in a word if he tried.

"I feel I've learned more about teaching in these few months than I did during my four years of college. I look back and cringe at some of my mistakes early on. I just wish I could have a do-over or something. But hey, a two week break and the start of a new semester are about as close as I can get, so I'll take it."

"I'm sure, Sheri, you'll do a wonderful job," assured Kris. "You'll keep building on all your progress from before the break."

"For me," voiced Trisha, "I've got some reworking of my lesson plans to do. I've now got a good idea of my class's strengths and weaknesses, so I've got to adjust my pacing a little. I'm also looking forward to doing more tutoring which I just started before the break. I've identified several students who I think could really take off with a little more individual attention."

"I'll be interested to hear how that goes," replied Kris, thoroughly enjoying the positive company. "For me, I'm planning to spend more time with my eighth graders in academic counseling. High school is right around the corner, and I fear that many are not quite prepared for the transition."

Mr. Phippen perked up from behind his sub-sandwich, as long and skinny as he. "You be sure to, uh… let me know how I can help you with that. I spent my first few teaching years at a high school, so I know, uh… I've got a good idea of what to expect."

"How gracious of you! Yes, I could use a little guidance on conducting transition meetings and course selection. I've still got to wrap my head around all those graduation requirements."

The group all smiled at Kris's willing acknowledgement. Despite her vast knowledge and experience, she was never too proud to admit areas of needed improvement. To them, she was like nature, always finding ways to grow.

Kris continued, "What about you, Paul? You asked the question, so you must have an answer."

"You know, I'm just ready to start teaching again. I believe I've taken a little more than a two week hiatus. It's about time I start doing a little better at fulfilling my job title."

Sheri, never too shy, brought the round of questioning full circle. "What about you Mr. Phippen? Do you have any goals for the rest of the year?"

"Oh, I, uh… I've got a few. But to tell you truth, my biggest resolution, uh… goal is to get in better shape. I've put on some weight, uh… a few pounds since August."

Surprised, each friend looked around at the group, their puzzled expressions confirming their collective confusion. What? The toothpick is watching his weight? Sheri, ever the bold one, voiced what they were all thinking.

"You, Mr. Phippen, have put on weight? Is that even possible?"

"I've been a little surprised too," answered the beanpole as he tossed in the last bite of lunch. "I've realized I need to watch, uh… lower my sugar intake. Lately, I can't seem to get enough candy, especially KitKats."

Counselor Kris's Cliff Notes
The Guiding Principles of Culture Creating

PRINCIPLE 1: High Expectations

1.1 *Defining Expectations*
   1.1.1 *Overview*
- Students generally perform to the level of their own expectations, whether high or low. As teachers cannot force students to hold themselves to certain expectations, teachers can, however, guide students to adopt those of the teacher. Expectations should be near the outer edge of, what researchers call, a student's *zone of proximal development (ZPD)*. Simply put, this means to set expectations high enough to be challenging but low enough to be attainable. When in doubt, err on the high side; students can perform at a much higher level than are often given credit.
- Define both behavioral and academic expectations.
- Avoid the term "rule" because of its negative connotation. The term "expectation" is more instructive and motivating by nature. It creates a sense of safety and community instead of authority and subordination.

   1.1.2 *Expectations vs. Standards vs. Procedures*
- <u>Expectations</u> are the *general ideals* to which students strive to achieve based on their *individual* abilities. They are the umbrella under which specific standards function. Terms are generally abstract so as to be more encompassing.
  - Behavioral Example – Respect your teacher and classmates.
  - Academic Example – Do your best work.
- <u>Standards</u> are the *specific minimums* to which *all students* must conform. They relate to an expectation, and they facilitate procedures.

Terms are specific and defined, usually beginning with a concrete action verb.
- Behavioral Example – Raise your hand to speak.
- Academic Example – Complete all your homework.

- <u>Procedures</u> are the prescribed *processes* all students follow to accomplish a specific standard or simplify and quicken the pace of class. Terms are specific and detailed, leaving no room for misinterpretation.
    - Behavioral Example – Raise your index finger for a question or your pinky for a comment.
    - Academic Example – Turn homework into the group leader who places all assignments in the designated tray.

1.2 *Communicating Expectations*

1.2.1. *Introducing Expectations*
- Two or three clear, concise expectations may be posted on the classroom wall. There is no need to post standards or procedures, for they are represented by the expectations. Plus, there will be too many, which will dilute the effect.
- Within the first week of school, teach all expectations, standards, and procedures *explicitly*. Do not assume that students know what is expected. Communicate them in plain terms through modeling, discussion, and practice.
- Introducing expectations, standards, and procedures can be done quickly, within the flow of instruction, and without becoming overwhelming. Select a few each day, teach them quickly, and move on to the day's content lesson. Then, when introducing a few the next day, begin with a quick review of those previously introduced.

1.2.2. *Reviewing Expectations*
- For the first period of time after all expectations, standards, and procedures have been introduced, regularly take time to review a

- few. This is a preventative measure that solidifies the concepts in long term memory.
- Thereafter and throughout the duration of the school year, occasionally discuss together the purpose of expectations, standards, and procedures as a source of reflection and application. Do not do so as a reaction to a breach; instead, do so in a positive manner, complimenting students on living up to the expectations.
- This process, over time, causes *your* expectations of *them* to become *their* expectations of *themselves*.

1.3 *Following Through on Expectations*
  1.3.1. *When Students Breach a Standard or Procedure*
- <u>Consistency</u>: Always follow through on standards and procedures. For instance, if you have a standard for students to raise their hand to speak and a student blurts out an answer, don't accept it. If you do, you're breaking your own standard and therefore reinforcing the very behavior you're trying to prevent. If there is a time it is permissible for the standard to be broken (i.e. speaking without raising hands during a group discussion), specifically tell students the beginning *and ending* of the allowable breach of the standard.
- <u>Methods</u>: There are numerous worthwhile methods to use when addressing students who breach standards and procedures: eye contact, proximity, reminders, warning systems, etc. Section 3.5 of these cliff notes outlines another worthwhile method. Yet in the end, the particular method used is not nearly as important as the fact that you use it consistently, following through with regularity.
- <u>Pacing</u>: Quick transitions and lesson pacing avoid lag time where breaches in standards and procedures are more likely to occur. Such high academic practices reinforce high behavioral expectations. Furthermore, be quick when addressing breached standards and procedures. Elongated lectures produce the opposite of the desired effect. Pre-plan strategies in order to implement them swiftly.

1.3.2. *When Students Breach an Expectation*
- Explanation: By definition, breached standards and procedures are breached expectations. However, in reality, a student who forgets their homework a single time isn't necessarily choosing a life path of failure. Yet, a student consistently doing so may be, and is thus guilty of breaching an expectation. Therefore, a student breaches expectations when *consistently* breaching standards or procedures or doing so a singular time in a *significant* way.
- Response: It is a big deal when expectations are breached. Wise and immediate intervention is needed, such as behavior trackers, parent meetings, or office intervention, to name a few. The method of intervention should be given in accordance with the other three guiding principles of culture creating.

PRINCIPLE 2: Relationships of Respect and Trust

2.1 *Definition and Purpose* – Teacher-student relationships of respect and trust provide the necessary motivation for a student to raise their personal expectations. The cords that permit a teacher to lead students are only as strong as their relationship. Therefore, it behooves teachers to cultivate the relationship necessary to create the environment in which students are willing and eager to follow, thus raising their personal expectations.

2.2 *Individual Interactions*

2.2.1. *Professional Approach* - Students generally perform to the measure of their immediate environment, whether high or low; therefore, teachers should approach their position at an even higher standard than they expect of their students. The teacher must be the consummate and consistent example. Be timely in your grading, be thorough in your feedback, and be available for discussion. Ensure your classroom is neat, welcoming, and organized. Maximize instructional time. Ensure students address you in respectful terms, usually by Mr. or Mrs. Dress and groom yourself in a manner that reflects the spirit of your classroom

expectations. Such a professional approach will demonstrate to students your commitment to your position and thus your respect for their time and confidence in their efforts. Teachers honor students when they honor their profession.

2.2.2. *Friends vs. Friendly* – Efforts to be professional should not result in a stiff, business-like approach. Kids are kids, and they relate better with those who are friendly. However, in striving to add friendliness to professionalism, a teacher may easily slip too far and interact similarly to that of a friend. For a teacher, it is possible to be professional and friendly, but it is not possible to be professional and friends. One must be on higher ground to lift another up.

- Friends – Interacts as a peer or equal. Has low expectations. Doesn't hold students accountable. Portrays oneself as cool, funny, and/or modern. Prioritizes being well-liked over student success.
- Friendly – Interacts as a willing mentor. Has high expectations. Holds students accountable. Is warm, welcoming, happy, and approachable. Builds relationships with students that lead to the ultimate goal of their success. Encourages and celebrates student success.

2.2.3. *Quadruple-P Interactions* – To build individual relationships, a teacher must have individual interactions with students within the normal context of school. If a student is treated as just one of the masses, the relationship (or lack thereof) will reflect it. Yet, when treated as the exceptional individual that they are, the cords of respect and trust will strengthen. Thus, teachers should routinely seek out ways to interact with individual students. The following "Quadruple-P" model optimizes such interactions.

- Purposeful – Deliberately seek out opportunities for interaction.
- Personalized – Take an interest in the interests of students. Find out what's important to them and share in the joy of their individual successes.
- Positive – Avoid teasing and sarcasm, as such comments may be misunderstood. Instead, compliment, uplift, and celebrate together.

- <u>P</u>rofessional – Avoid all semblance of foul play. All personal interactions should be done with the distinct feel of an interested mentor.
- EXAMPLE IDEAS
    - Brief hallway conversation
    - In class compliment
    - Short, personal note
    - Postcard sent home
    - Parental contact for the sole purpose of complimenting their child

2.3 *Intrinsic vs. Extrinsic Motivation*

    2.3.1 *Motivation and Relationships* – A classroom culture of success is predicated upon students' motivation to follow their teacher and seek success. The strength of motivation directly correlates with the strength of the teacher-student relationship. Thus, building the relationship and employing proper methods of motivation strengthen the classroom culture.

    2.3.2 *Definitions*

- <u>Extrinsic Motivation</u> – Working to accomplish a goal for the purpose of receiving an external reward (i.e. pizza party, free time, avoiding a punishment). This may produce desired results in the short term, but it does not build long term, sustainable self-motivation.
- <u>Intrinsic Motivation</u> – Working to accomplish a goal for the purpose of receiving an internal reward (i.e. knowledge, personal satisfaction, sense of accomplishment). This may produce desired results in the short term but will most certainly create long term, sustainable self-motivation.

    2.3.3 *Methods to Build Intrinsic Motivation*

1. <u>Set Appropriate and Meaningful Expectations</u> – Expectations should be on the outer edge of an individual student's ZPD, providing an attainable challenge. This makes success possible, for if expectations are too high, they are unreachable, and if too low, accomplishing them is not true success.

2. Dynamic Presentation – Present material in a manner that engages students' interest. Teach with enthusiasm. Connect material to students' personal lives. Present admirable examples and models. Allow for a variety of ways for students to demonstrate their learning.
3. Self-Monitoring – Teach students to be their own best critics, not to the point of self-depreciation, but instead to help themselves rise to their own expectations. Teach methods to properly self-monitor, such as rubrics, checklists, and time to self-analyze.
4. Positive Encouragement and Recognition – Regularly praise the progress and accomplishments of students. Celebrate individual and class successes together. Recognize effort; help students see the connection between work and success.
5. Sharing Accomplishments – Create opportunities for students to share their accomplishments. This can be done in class (i.e. explaining their favorite part of a project to the class), or this can be done outside of class time (i.e. signing a poster or posting exceptional work on walls). When done well, the time this takes is worth tenfold in building intrinsic value.
6. Extrinsic Hook – Though the above strategies work in most instances, occasionally students need something else for a kick start. On these exceptional occasions, offer a worthwhile yet small extrinsic hook to get them moving in the right direction. Then, wean students away as quickly as possible to avoid enabling dependence.

PRINCIPLE 3: Reinforce the Positive

3.1 *Definition* – Psychology's definition of "positive reinforcement" involves *adding* a stimulus to a student behavior to make it more likely to recur, such as *adding* a written "well done" at the top of a spelling test. A poor use of positive reinforcement is adding to or recognizing undesired behavior, such as laughing at a student's off-topic joke. Hence, teachers should not only positively reinforce, they should *reinforce the positive*, thereby increasing the likelihood of it being repeated and thus strengthening the classroom culture as a whole.

3.2 *Purpose* – A classroom culture of success is laser focused on learning and achieving, and is therefore devoid of other distractions, including inappropriate student behavior. Student success is more likely to be achieved when the classroom culture is such that students want to behave appropriately. They understand what is *expected* of them, they *respect* and *trust* their teacher, and they're encompassed by an environment that is *safe, positive,* and *appreciative of good behavior.* Therefore, managing student behavior by reinforcing the positive, as outlined in the following three-pronged model, eliminates this distraction and enables focus on learning and achieving.

3.3 *Prong One: Ignore Inconsequential Behavior* – Most student behaviors, even misbehaviors, can simply be ignored. Harping on every little whisper and pencil tap creates a sense of authoritarianism and may actually reinforce the very behavior you're striving to eliminate. Though you may win the battle by temporarily stopping such behaviors, you lose the overall war of creating a culture of success, so choose your battles wisely. Step back and keep the big picture in mind. Many inappropriate student behaviors are simply inconsequential, where the greater consequence is to actually address them. Therefore, it behooves a teacher to identify that which is consequential, address them as outlined in the next two prongs, and then ignore all the rest.

3.4 *Prong Two: Recognize Desired Behavior* – Students generally do that which receives attention, especially from a respected and trusted adult. So when a teacher attends to a misbehavior, the student received the attention they sought and are therefore more likely to do it again. Teachers should instead use the opposite approach and attend to desired behavior, which will increase the likelihood of the desired behavior's recurrence.

    3.4.1. *To Redirect Undesired Behavior* – One method to stop undesired behavior is to ignore it, as stated in 3.3, and then redirect it through recognizing the desired behavior of another. Oft times the student, who wants the attention of the respected teacher, will then comply of their own accord. The teacher should soon thereafter individually recognize that student for conforming to the expectation. This process redirects undesired behavior without ever addressing it, and culminates with a relationship strengthening interaction.

3.4.2. *Habits and Culture* – Purposefully and dutifully develop the habit of speaking positively with students. The warmth of your countenance and kindness of your words strengthens relationships and empowers students to reach high to achieve the expectations. Develop the habit of regularly recognizing both the class as a whole and students as individuals. With each sincere compliment, recognition, and word of praise, your habits will change and your culture of success will strengthen.

3.5 *Prong Three: Properly Address Consequential Misbehavior* – Despite your best efforts to ignore inconsequential behavior and recognize desired behavior, there will be times when students misbehave to the point where it must be addressed, where failing to do so would blur expectations and weaken culture. And while there are some major infractions that necessitate severe intervention (office referrals, etc.), most misbehavior can and should be addressed by the teacher. Doing so maintains authority and strengthens relationships. The moment misbehaviors are addressed is significant. Addressing the student improperly may cause harm, where doing so as outlined below will not only avoid the harm but also strengthen the relationship.

3.5.1. *Principles of Addressing Consequential Misbehavior*
- Maintain the dignity of the student. Never demean or belittle; instead build and strengthen. Treat the student as they may become, remembering they only briefly forgot their own expectations and potential.
- Address the behavior as privately as possible. This helps maintain the student's dignity and limits the peer attention some may seek.

- Enable the student to do as much of the talking as possible. Lectures have minimal impact where effective questioning will more likely produce desired outcomes.

3.5.2. *The Three Question Model* – Help students accept responsibility for their own behavior through helping them vocalize the following three items. Then, end the conversation by expressing confidence that they can fulfill their plan and rise to the expectations.

- <u>What</u> did I do wrong? (The infraction)
- <u>Why</u> was it wrong? (The expectation they breached)
- <u>How</u> do I plan to fix it? (Realigning behavior to expectations)

PRINCIPLE 4: Student-Centered Instruction

4.1 *Overview and Purpose* – The first three principles prepare the way for teachers to do what they do best – teach. They enable teachers to take full advantage of classroom instructional time, for students are then fully engaged, focused, and motivated to learn and achieve. So, with the class culture ripe for learning, the teacher must then capitalize by teaching the content in a manner most likely to achieve success – student-centered instruction.

4.2 *Definitions: Lesson-Centered vs. Self-Centered vs. Student-Centered*

4.2.1. *Lesson-Centered Instruction*

- <u>Primary Focus</u> – Delivering a quality presentation.
- <u>Ultimate Goal</u> – Engaging students in the process of the learning activity.
- <u>Methods</u> – As lesson-centered teachers primarily focus on the process, they put their energies toward creating fun and engaging methods of lesson delivery while neglecting the ultimate purpose of that very lesson. They seek the "wow-factor" more than student achievement. They do not consider the learning needs of individual students because they care more for the positive reaction of the whole.

4.2.2. *Self-Centered Instruction*
- <u>Primary Focus</u> – Teaching in a manner that fulfills one's own objectives.
- <u>Ultimate Goal</u> – Fulfilling one's own needs at the possible expense of students.
- <u>Methods</u> – A self-centered teacher's objective is sometimes personal recognition, but more often than not, their methodology demonstrates that to them teaching is "just a job." When lesson planning, they do not consider the unique needs of their class, often using the same lesson plans each year or doing exactly as the textbook outlines. They do not accommodate individual needs. Their lesson delivery is methodical and inflexible. They may be selfish with curricula, schedules, and other school-related functions. Whether they recognize it in themselves or not, they prioritize themselves over students.

4.2.3. *Student-Centered Instruction*
- <u>Primary Focus</u> – Guiding students to achieve according to their individual circumstances.
- <u>Ultimate Goal</u> – Individual student success.
- <u>Methods</u> – A student-centered teacher focuses on individual students and tailors instruction to the unique needs of each class. These teachers employ engaging lessons for the purpose of learning concepts. They are willing and able to flex from lesson plans according to student needs. They accommodate individuals through modified assignments, tutoring, or other means, despite the additional effort necessary to do so. They are data driven. They are willing learners. They are team players amongst faculty members, able and willing to share and sacrifice for the good of the whole. Their priorities place students above themselves.

4.3 *Application of the Principle of Student-Centered Instruction* – As there are as many applications of student-centered instruction as there are students, it is impossible to outline concrete techniques that could be universally applied. In fact, it shouldn't even be attempted, for doing so would ultimately fail at least some small sector of students. As direct instruction may work well for one, discovery learning may be better for another. Where some flourish with group work, others need independent study. Where some are auditory learners, others are visual, or logical, or kinesthetic. It is, therefore, the duty of the student-centered teacher to assess the overall needs of the class, tailor the general instruction to them, and then work to accommodate the needs of the outliers. This approach meets the needs of all students and provides them the best possible opportunity to choose the path of success for themselves.

About the Author

Nathan Cureton is a passionate educator, author, trainer, and leader. With teaching experience ranging from middle school to university, leadership experience ranging from elementary to high school, and undergrad and graduate degrees in teaching and educational leadership, Nathan's entire professional world has been wrapped up in creating successful classrooms. Best known for his charismatic teaching and dedication to student success, the title he most prefers is that singularly noble word – teacher.

Nathan's school leadership experience began with a striking resemblance to East Crossroad's own Mr. Phippen, or so his mind has embellished. Yet, with experience and opportunity came growth and success. Nathan later enjoyed serving in numerous teacher development activities at his own school and beyond. Known for his engaging wit, dynamic instruction, and motivating style, Nathan's influence continues to spread throughout the education community, influencing both teacher and student alike.

Nathan now resides in northern Utah with his wife and four children, the foundation of his motivation.

Made in the USA
Charleston, SC
25 April 2015